*The Correspondence of Ezra Pound
and Senator William Borah*

The Correspondence of Ezra Pound and Senator William Borah

Edited by
Sarah C. Holmes

Foreword by
Daniel Pearlman

University of Illinois Press
Urbana and Chicago

© 2001 by the Board of Trustees
of the University of Illinois
All rights reserved
Manufactured in the United States of
America
∞ This book is printed on
acid-free paper.

Library of Congress
Cataloging-in-Publication Data
Pound, Ezra, 1885–1972.
[Correspondence. Selections]
The correspondence of Ezra Pound
and Senator William Borah / edited by
Sarah C. Holmes ; foreword by Daniel
Pearlman.
p. cm.
Includes bibliographical references
and index.
ISBN 0-252-02630-6 (alk. paper)
1. Pound, Ezra, 1885–1972—
Correspondence. 2. Poets,
American—20th century—
Correspondence. 3. Borah, William
Edgar, 1865–1940—Correspondence.
4. Legislators—United States—
Correspondence. I. Borah, William
Edgar, 1865–1940. II. Holmes, Sarah.
III. Title.
PS3531.O82Z4817   2001
811'.52—dc21   00-010325
C 5 4 3 2 1

Contents

ACKNOWLEDGMENTS vii
FOREWORD BY DANIEL PEARLMAN ix
NOTE ON THE TEXT xi
INTRODUCTION xv
THE LETTERS 1
APPENDIXES
A. Related Letters 71
B. The Meeting between the Poet and the Senator 79
WORKS CITED 85
INDEX 91

Acknowledgments

There are many people to thank for their help with this project. They include Barry Ahearn and the 1997 MLA panel (who heard a version of my introduction), Jamie Carr, Michael G. Cornelius, Lois Cuddy, Dorothy Donnelly, James Findlay, the Holmes family, Michael Honhart, Kristen Kennedy, Robert Kibler, Maury Klein, Susan Peterson, the scholars on the Pound e-mail list, Andrée Rathemacher, Willis Regier, Ted Shear, the late Dana Shugar, Paschal Viglionese, and Oliver Zeltner.

I also thank the following for their permission to publish these letters: Charles E. Corker, Mary de Rachewiltz, Omar S. Pound, Mary Schedler, and Declan Spring.

Finally, I thank Dan Pearlman for being an intelligent, encouraging, and amazingly generous mentor.

Foreword

DANIEL PEARLMAN

    In 1979, when I was chair of the English department at the University of Idaho, I had the good fortune to be able to fund the visits of Marshall McLuhan and Ezra Pound's daughter, Mary de Rachewiltz, for the annual Pound Lecture (a short-lived tradition, unfortunately). During that visit, Mary suggested that I edit a correspondence—of whose existence I had been unaware—between her father and the erstwhile Idaho senator William E. Borah. Although I was happy to undertake the task, a career change forced me to lay it indefinitely aside—and the project would have continued in limbo if not for my doctoral student Sarah Holmes, who has proved to have the perfect combination of skill and enthusiasm to get the job properly done.

  This correspondence reveals a minor drama in which an overly self-confident poet, whom Gertrude Stein had called a "village explainer," attempts throughout the tumultuous decade of the thirties to educate, for the role of the presidency, the one Republican statesman he believed could beat Roosevelt if nominated by his party. Pound clearly hoped to be a king-maker of a sort, a gray eminence who would supply Borah with the savvy needed to beat FDR and successfully end the Great Depression while also keeping the United States out of a looming European war.

  Looking back at this correspondence from our millennial perspective, we see a dark comedy unfold: an arrogant Pound lecturing, in the tone of a crackerbox philosopher, to a polite but largely unresponsive senator on politics and economics. We feel the mounting frustration of the expatriate poet as he badgers and hectors Borah in a quirky, colloquial, overly familiar tone that obviously did not go down well with the senator, who upon eventually meeting Pound wondered if this ex-Idahoan was literally "crazy." Even as we smile, we can't help feeling sorry for a pathetic Pound frantically pursuing his self-appointed mission to save the world through his anointed surrogate, the Republican senator from Idaho. Even Borah's failure to achieve his party's nomination for the 1936 election did not stop the driven poet from hoping for the senator's triumph come 1940—although it was clear from Borah's late-thirties speeches that he had become, unlike Pound, decidedly antifascist. Borah's death in 1940 punctured that balloon. And Pearl Harbor punctured all of Pound's earlier hope.

Note on the Text

The correspondence between Ezra Pound (1885–1972) and William Borah (1865–1940) lasted from 1933 to 1939 and consists of thirty-one extant letters, twenty-eight from Pound and three from Borah. The appendixes contain additional letters related to this correspondence. The letters examined are either carbon copies or later versions. Pound typed each of his letters over a piece of carbon paper and would often make changes to the original letter but not to the carbon. He would then send the corrected letter to his correspondent. Therefore, a carbon found at one archive may be different from the original held in another location. In some cases, I had access to both the carbon copy and the original. If the original was not available, I relied on the carbon copy alone. The reader should note that although Pound made changes to his letters, he did not correct many of his grammatical oddities and misspellings.

Pound's letters can be found in the Yale Collection of American Literature at the Beinecke Rare Book and Manuscript Library at Yale University and at the Library of Congress. Most of the letters included in this volume are held in the Ezra Pound Papers at the Beinecke Library and are in the Borah, Sen. William E. (1933–39) file, folders 218–19, box 5, series 1, general correspondence. Pound's letter to Clarence A. Bottolfsen, included in appendix A, is in this file. Letter 6 is in the Cutting, Bronson Murray (1930–35) file in folders 507–8, box 11. (The letter was sent to Cutting, but it may have been sent to Borah also.)

Pound's letter to George Tinkham, included in appendix A, is in the Tinkham, George Holden (1933–41, 1959) file in folders 2361–74, box 52. Letters 1, 5, 7, 8, 11, 17, 18, 19, 28, and Homer Pound's letter to Borah included in appendix A were found at the Library of Congress in the Papers of William Edgar Borah, 1905–40. Copies of letters 1, 7, 8, 11, and 28 are at both the Beinecke Library and the Library of Congress. Letter 28, however, has two different dates (13 March 1936 on the Beinecke Library's copy and 12 March 1936 on the Library of Congress's copy). Letter 19, a holograph letter few Poundians are aware of, is in a file marked "For. Aff. Misc. May-Nov. 1935" in the Borah papers at the Library of Congress. All of Borah's letters (letters 2, 9, and 20) are in his collection of correspondence at the Library of Congress and also at the Beinecke Library. The letter from Charles A. Corker to Daniel Pearlman included in appendix B is in Pearlman's possession.

Wyndham Lewis has commented that "E.P.'s letters tidied up would no longer be E.P.'s letters" (qtd. in Ahearn x). Indeed, I have reproduced the original flavor of Pound's letters as much as possible but have made some minor concessions to readability.

Each letter is tagged with an abbreviation describing its physical form. For example, "TLS-2" indicates a typed letter signed by the author that consists of two pages. "AL-1" indicates a one-page autograph letter that is unsigned. This tag is immediately followed by the place of composition, which was usually indicated by the correspondent's letterhead. If I am uncertain of a letter's origin, the place name appears in brackets.

Because it is fairly consistent, I have not included the wording of the letterhead either correspondent used. A few of Pound's letters were written on blank paper, but the majority were on his "E. Pound / Rapallo" letterhead. All of Borah's letters were typed on "United States Senate / Committee on Foreign Relations" letterhead.

I have standardized the placement and format of dates. Most letters were dated by the correspondents, but occasionally I have had to make an estimate based on internal evidence. When I have had to supply the date I have put the information in brackets. For example, "2 January [1936]" indicates that the letter was written on the second of January, as indicated by the correspondent, but I am not certain of the year. Occasionally the correspondent included an address or other information at the top of the letter. Each of these has been reproduced as written or typed in the original but all locations have been regularized.

I have not attempted to reproduce the exact layout of Pound's letters. Hugh Witemeyer reminds us that Pound's idiosyncratic spacing cannot be reproduced accurately except in a facsimile edition (xii). Simply put, Pound sometimes uses so many characters to a line that the only way to reproduce such lines in proportion to their margins would be to shrink the type or use an oversize page. Because I have opted for ordinary margins, type, and pages, Pound's exact spacing and formatting cannot be duplicated. Therefore, headings, salutations, and closings appear in only the same general locations as in the original letters. I have regularized the spacing between lines, even though at times Pound double-spaces a letter and then begins single-spacing it halfway through. I have omitted extra spacing between words and sentences and have eliminated the spaces separating marks of punctuation from words.

I have not reproduced Pound's exact paragraph indentions but have instead regularized them. When Pound skips a line to indicate a paragraph break, I have inserted an indention instead and have closed up the lines. In some letters Pound moves down a line but still seems to be working within the same paragraph. I have silently merged lines that seem to belong to a single paragraph.

I have copied Pound's typographical irregularities as much as possible. Pound's underlining—though occasionally halting in the middle of a word—appears in this volume as it does in his letters. All erratic capitalization has been reproduced, so words that begin sentences are not always capitalized and sometimes a capital letter will appear in the middle of a word. For clarity, I have changed Pound's equal signs to either hyphens or em-dashes, depending on the context.

I have reproduced all of Pound's misspellings and typographical errors. He often spelled words incorrectly, and he often spelled the same word differently in the same letter (e.g., VanBuren and Van Buren appear together). The reader can be assured that any misspelled word or typographical oddity occurs in the original letter, including those written by Borah and those in the appendixes. Annotations, where they appear, will always provide the correct spelling.

Pound's substantive handwritten and typed insertions are enclosed in angle brackets (< >). Minor insertions, such as "a" or "the," have been silently added to the text. I have omitted illegible or insignificant material Pound crossed out. Although the letters are filled with "HHHHH" across other characters, such deletions have not been included here. Even with his erratic style and habit of correcting his letters by hand, few words are unreadable. Such places in the text are indicated by "[?]."

The letters are reproduced in their entirety, so all ellipses belong to Pound. On occasion Pound did not get the carbon paper inserted in his typewriter correctly and a line or two was lost. I indicate these instances by the editorial designation "[line(s) missing]."

Annotations are provided in notes immediately following each letter. Most issues recur throughout the correspondence, although Pound may emphasize first one person's role and then another's. I have offered lengthy commentary for the most significant people or concepts. I have also provided glosses for obscure or cryptic references, clarified Pound's thinking, or indicated Borah's thoughts when Pound raises an issue. In some instances, I have opted to let minor subjects pass without comment so as to have a less cluttered text.

Introduction

In 1979, Mary de Rachewiltz, Ezra Pound's daughter, suggested to Daniel Pearlman that he publish the correspondence between her father and Senator William Borah of Idaho. Pearlman was delighted to learn of the letters and soon obtained the entire correspondence and the permission to publish it. Seventeen years later, when I met Pearlman, the project was still sitting on the back burner. When he asked me if I would be interested in editing the letters, I welcomed the opportunity to be mentored by a gifted Pound scholar and to learn about the turbulent thirties through the eyes of two influential players in American history. A colleague once asked me to provide three words to describe this correspondence. My response: "chaotic, weird, and . . . fascinating."

Any student of Pound knows that his letters are unusual because he simultaneously reveres and insults the people to whom he is writing while making references to obscure people and events of which his correspondents are frequently unaware. The correspondence between Pound and Borah reflects all these characteristics, but more importantly it opens up a window into the mind of someone living in the midst of great turmoil. During the thirties, Roosevelt made a New Deal, economic experts thought they could save or abolish the gold standard, radical theories such as Austria's stamp scrip were catching the attention of senators in the United States, the Italian invasion of Abyssinia sent the League of Nations into an uproar, two presidential elections took place, and the world moved closer and closer to war. From "far away" Rapallo, Italy, Ezra Pound watched, listened, and tried to change the world by writing to hundreds of politicians, from Mussolini to Borah (Pound, "From" 38). Although Borah never took Pound seriously, the letters Pound wrote to him, which date from 1933 to 1939, can further educate Pound scholars about how the poet interpreted one of the most turbulent and exciting times in recent world history.

Pound wrote extensively about alternate economic theories, some radical, some seriously weighed by mainstream politicians. One persistent idea circulating at the time was Social Credit. According to this theory, private banks charged so much interest for the use of their credit and money that prices of goods were always higher than consumers could afford. Because consumers could not buy the goods they needed, poverty resulted even though countries had surplus goods. Simply put, a country that overproduces needs to give purchasing power to more than just the elite in order to sell the goods it has made and thus keep money circulating. Social Credit was a plan to put the control of credit into the hands of the government, which would also distribute a dividend to the public and thereby allow consumers to purchase more goods (Walkiewicz and Witemeyer 6–7). Pound first met one of Social Credit's founders, Major C. H. Douglas, in 1918—a meeting that would change Pound's life and have a dramatic effect on his writings.

Throughout his letters to Borah, Pound refers to many Social Credit tenets as well as to the bankers he blamed for the worldwide economic depression. Pound argues that bankers should have less control over money—thereby making less profit—and that the people needed purchasing power. On 15 May 1934 Pound writes, "Every factory, every industry, under the preset shitten and snotten system <u>produces prices FASTER than it emits the power to buy</u>" (letter 8). Such concerns were not merely idiosyncratic but were rather on the minds of people around the world. As the literary scholar Tim Redman notes, many argued at the time that if domestic markets could not suffice, a nation would be forced to compete in international markets, causing the competition and exploitation that would lead to world war (59).

In 1934, in the early stages of his correspondence with Borah, Pound became familiar with the theories of Silvio Gesell, a German businessman who advocated the use of stamp scrip (Redman 126). In 1932, the mayor of the small Austrian village of Wörgl adopted Gesellian economics and began a controversial experiment. Approximately one-third of the workers were employees of a public works project and were paid in stamp scrip. Each note of currency was stamped once a month at a rate of 1 percent of its face value. Each stamp therefore decreased the original value of the note, and if a person held on to the note long enough, the accumulated stamps would cancel out the original value. It was a successful plan while it lasted and increased the circulation of money (Redman 127–29). After the Austrian National Bank brought a lawsuit against the town for infringing on its monopoly, however, the experiment came to a close. Because Pound saw stamp scrip as a way to solve the circulation problems with which Social Credit was concerned, he proclaimed its benefits to Borah. In his letter of 15 January 1934, he cajoles, "Come on, be decent, if the govt. is blowing 40 billion, pay out 50 million in stamp scrip. What the HELL is the use trying to hide the fact that it works. Woergl demonstration. WORKED" (letter 3).

Although primary in emphasis, Pound's ideas about alternative economic theories are only part of what we reap from his letters to Borah. Throughout the letters we see a nervous struggle between the two men. Borah finds Pound's geographical position problematic, and Pound was insecure about his ability to solve his homeland's problems from his self-exile in Italy. In fact, the tension over exile emerges as the most pervasive thread in the correspondence. Philip J. Burns argues that Pound was delusional in believing that his letters to politicians would be taken seriously and cites Pound's fervent attempts to persuade Borah to adopt his way of thinking as an example of this delusion. Throughout these letters, however, Pound tries to compensate for his awkward position as an expatriate in Italy. Many times Pound refers to his expatriation and therefore clearly understands his precarious position. Regardless of their shared distrust of powerful businesses and monopolies, Pound knew that he had to work hard to sell Borah on his alternative economic ideas. One might speculate that this is why he wrote so many letters—Pound knew he had a difficult sale to make. Thus, the letters are fascinating if for no other reason than that they reveal Pound's attempt to claim authority and give advice about American politics in spite of his long-term residence abroad.

Pound does attempt to maneuver himself out of expatriation. In his first letter to Borah he begins, "As an Idahoan, it wd. interest me to know whether your ignorance of the Bankhead bill is real or pretended." As Daniel Pearlman suggests, Pound uses his birthplace as a selling point to the Republican senator of that state (Pearlman 420). Borah's assistant clerk, Charles E. Corker, remarks that "Borah was always accessible to Idahoans" and that "he followed a rule that no Idahoan ever expatriated himself, even if he moved to Italy, which accounts for why he found time to see Pound" (see appendix B). In contrast, Borah (or one of his staff members, as Corker points out) begins his first letter to Pound with the recommendation that Pound return to the States: "'As an Idahoan' I suggest that you come back to Idaho and to the United States. It isn't fair to give us so much 'hell' at so great a distance. I can talk better than I can write. So drop in when you get home and see me" (letter 2).

Despite his repeated exhortations, Pound's attempt to convert Borah failed. The senator was not willing to respond to his fervent claims about American politics—even if he was born in Idaho. In the face of dozens of letters Pound wrote over six years, Borah did not address the issues Pound raised but instead made remarks about the physical distance between the two men. In his second letter, Borah asks when Pound will return to Idaho, and in his final letter, he tells Pound about the weather.

Pound, however, continues his argument with Borah over the geography of politics and comments that Borah is in no position to place emphasis on geography. In a letter dated 24 March 1934, Pound scolds: "It is all very well for you to suggest that I could curse more effectively if I were in Idaho or Washington. I am not sure of it. If I knew any was of getting Farley out of the District of Columbia or preventing people with no more intelligence than HULL from being appointed to positions demanding at least the barins of street car conductor, I might risk the boat fare" (letter 4). In an earlier letter, he chastises Borah severely: "Don' you talk to me about Geography. When you think of the foreign countryies you have AUTHORITY'D, without knowing whether they were in Europe Asia or Afrikaaa!!!" (letter 3). Indeed, Pound makes an excellent point. Others had questioned Borah's refusal to travel to Europe, especially since he was chairman of the Senate Foreign Relations Committee. Borah responded to his critics:, "I should add little to my knowledge by infrequent brief trips to Europe. It is often wiser to stand off and obtain a clear picture. One might become merely confused by first-hand information" (qtd. in McKenna 220). Borah did not listen to Pound even though they shared this opinion about transatlantic politics, probably because he did not find Pound's ideas worth listening to.

Pound nevertheless persisted. His third attempt to maneuver out of his awkward position was to argue that he had a certain vantage point from which to look on European and American affairs. In a letter dated 15 January 1934 Pound claims, "That triple skink Wilson wd/ have saved time if he had got his *European* news from Americans in Europe rather than from Missouri" (letter 3). These words are revealing. First, Pound still considered himself an "American," regardless of his home in Italy; second, he was well aware that his correspondents might be harder to convince because of his expatriation; and third, being an American patriot in Italy was perfectly feasible. Indeed, he seemed to have successfully maneuvered himself out of a geographical position and into an ideological one. In a letter to Congressman George Tinkham, for example, he explains that he went to Italy "to see the difference between what blokes write in a high brow weekly and what gets DONE" (Burns 71), and in 1935 he complains to Borah, "Pity my knowledge of Europe can't be some use to the nation" (letter 24). Edward Said argues that "borders and barriers, which enclose us within the safety of familiar territory, can also become prisons, and are often defended beyond reason or necessity. Exiles cross borders, break barriers of thought and experience" (451). Pound may not have been delusional at all, but instead may have seen things more clearly from where he sat. Although Pound was not an exile but a self-exile, he did have some ability to "transcend national or provincial limits" and to achieve a "plurality of vision" comprehending two countries (Said 451–52). Pound had the advantage of reading Italian newspapers, which exaggerated the United States' neutrality as well as Italy's good works (Harris 47).

This perspective also worked to Pound's disadvantage. He apparently believed too much of what he read in the Italian papers and presumably accepted some of Mussolini's policies and actions based on the government's rationalizations. Pound thus needed to argue his position on Mussolini's invasion of Abyssinia especially vigorously. In this volume we see letters stating the poet's true convictions about this controversial subject. Although many scholars have denied or tried to minimize Pound's fascist politics, by doing so we take his poetry—especially the cantos from the 1930s—out of context. Tim Redman maintains that "we do ourselves a disservice by ignoring the frightening aspects of his allegiances or by attempting to somehow partition his life and work into the acceptable and the taboo" (1). These letters help scholars to better comprehend Pound as a political poet and his poetry as a political medium. Julia Kristeva contends that the poetry of the cantos "overcomes" their fascist ideology (qtd. in Redman 2). As readers will see in these letters, however, Pound uses the cantos as his arsenal to weaken Borah's convictions, to bring him over to Pound's side.

These letters between the poet and senator significantly broaden our understanding of how far Pound took his esteem for Mussolini. On 3 October 1935, Mussolini invaded Abyssinia. Italy and Abyssinia belonged to the League of Nations and many members of the league were certain this aggression would lead to another war. The league had an obligation to defend an invaded country, especially one that had requested its help, but was limited in its authority to punish a member nation. Sir Samuel Hoare of Great Britain assured the world that his country would use force if needed to contain Mussolini. After the invasion, the league imposed sanctions; regardless, Italy conquered the African country in 1936. Prior to the invasion, Pound writes, "The question of Abyssinia is NOT whether the league wants etc/ or don't want It is a question of whether ANY nation that doesn't crawl on its belly and take orders from London (from the most treacherous nation of earth) is to have the league used against it; is to suffer unlimited and unscrupulous blackmail, wangled by England" (1 Oct. 1935; letter 17). In the month following the invasion, Pound acknowledges that at first he interpreted the action as war and was "sorry" about the invasion but later realized that Italy was being unfairly judged (letter 21). In one of two previously unknown letters that he hurriedly hand-wrote to Borah immediately after the invasion, he is even more enthusiastic. On 10 October 1935 he insists that "7 million of subjected population in Abyssinia will be benefitted by conquest" (letter 18). He reminds Borah that Italy has made tremendous strides in improving the lives of its people and seems to suggest that its international policies will be successful because its domestic ones were.

Pound goes on in the letter to explain Mussolini's actions: "He has stopped war in Europe repeatedly: & I believe got it into Africa as alternative." In the *New English Weekly* issue of 21 November 1935, Pound notes that "American opinion seems to think Mussolini has got war out of Europe into a less deadly corner, or at least one less annihilative to civilization" (105). Outraged over the sanctions that would be imposed on Italy for its invasion, Pound suggests that England was once interested in obtaining Abyssinia and adds that "Chamberlain himself admits Abyssinia isn't civilized" (letter 22). Pound continues to warn Borah that sanctions would have adverse effects like restricting consumption, raising gas prices, and increasing munitions sales. In addition, he repeatedly suggests that Borah read chapters of his book *Jefferson and/or Mussolini* to understand his alignment with Mussolini's politics.

In spite of his zeal, Pound failed to convince Borah that he could understand the world from Rapallo. When he visited Borah in 1939, he was not warmly welcomed and wrote about the visit in canto 84: "'am sure I don't know what a man like you / would find to *do* here' / said Senator Borah." A letter from Borah's assistant clarifies Borah's impressions of the meeting. When Charles Corker drove Borah home on the day he spent twenty minutes listening to Pound, Borah made two remarks about this encounter: "Do you know how that poet makes a living?" and "I think he's crazy" (see appendix B). Hence we get a different reading of canto 84 if we remove the emphasis from the word *do* and place it elsewhere: "'am sure I don't know what a man *like you* / would find to do here' / said Senator Borah." Believing that his expatriation justified Borah's refusal to engage in a serious correspondence, as Borah seemed to suggest in his letters, Pound was unaware that Borah was simply not interested in his poetry or economic ideas.

Borah's views on fascism certainly illuminate his rejection of Pound's. On 17 May 1934 during a speech before the Senate, Borah remarked that "Fascism, Nazi-ism, Communism, appealing to the forces of terror and fanaticism, have submerged, buried, the individual beneath the schemes of personal aggrandizement. They have challenged democracy, and they have challenged democracy because democracy stands for free speech and personal liberty" ("Delegation" 17). It is obvious from this and other statements that Borah's emphasis on individual rights and his adherence to these opinions would have made it difficult for Pound to convince him of Mussolini's positive attributes. It is unfortunate that Borah never significantly addressed Pound's concerns because then we would have learned more about Borah.

From what we do know about the politician, it makes perfect sense that Pound would consider him a possible presidential candidate and spokesman for his platform. Borah was not only one of the most outspoken members of the Senate but also an accomplished and interesting character. After attending the University of Kansas, he moved to Boise, Idaho, to practice law. He participated in some notable criminal trials and then began a term in the Senate, where he supported bills that would establish the Department of Labor and the Children's Bureau. The Republican senator vehemently opposed the trusts, adopted a Jeffersonian philosophy of social reform, and opposed federal centralization ("Borah," *Concise*). The senator who rode his horse around the parks in urban Washington was also an independent thinker who caused some controversy. He voted inconsistently and disputed most of the Wilson administration's legislation. He denounced monopolies, high tariffs, bureaucracy, and great expenditures by candidates for office. Specifically, he started an inquiry into the excessive funds used to promote the presidential candidacies of Frank Lowden and Leonard Wood, thereby indirectly causing the nomination of Warren Harding.

Although he publicly announced that he would remain loyal to the Republican party, he favored too many progressive ideas to be of real use to William Taft as a vice presidential candidate. From the start, he was an unyielding senator. In 1911, for example, he opposed a treaty with Nicaragua that he considered an endorsement of imperialism and was the only Republican who voted against it. The treaty was defeated because of Borah's vote (Vinson 4–5).

He took great pride in his independent judgment. His favorite quotation was from Ralph Waldo Emerson: "It is easy in the world to live after the world's opinion; it is easy in solitude to live after your own; but the great man is he who in the midst of the crowd keeps with perfect sweetness the independence of solitude" (qtd. in Vinson 9). Borah felt that he was doing a great service by remaining free of partisan biases. Another of Borah's favorite quotes was Edmund Burke's view of public servants: "Your representative owes you not his industry only but his judgement. And he betrays instead of serving you if he sacrifices it to your opinion" (qtd. in Vinson 9). Borah's self-reliance was most likely a factor in Pound's choice of him as a potential spokesperson.

Borah was active in world politics and was known by all to have held strong convictions. He was one of the most unyielding opponents to the Treaty of Versailles when it was submitted to the Senate in 1919 and believed that entrance into the League of Nations would unnecessarily entangle the United States in world disputes. He contended that the only way to avoid war was to disarm, not to create a league for peace. On 22 September 1935, Borah made a radio speech demonstrating sympathy with some of Pound's views. In it Borah agrees that war in Europe seemed probable, but that it was only a means of realizing "vast profits" and expending "great sums" for "instruments fit only for the destruction of human beings" ("Senator" 3). He also advises the United States to stay out of other countries' affairs and "remain aloof from all foreign wars" (4).

In another radio address on 22 February 1936, Borah urges the United States to remain neutral and cites the controversy surrounding the Italian invasion of Abyssinia (which he refers to as Ethiopia) as a reason: "When the people of the United States determined to remain neutral in the Italian-Ethiopian war, and when they determine, as they will, to remain neutral in all European controversies, they will be acting in harmony with what they believe to be our national interests" ("Washington's" 6). Borah's main rhetorical strategy is to use the example of

Britain's neutrality when Japan invaded Manchuria. Great Britain's representative told the League of Nations that the country would remain neutral because that was in its best interest. Borah, who was known for his sharp rhetorical skills, asserts that even if the nations involved are in the League of Nations, there is still a precedent to follow national interest:

> And Great Britain having declared that it was to her interests to remain neutral, under what rule of international sanity or of national responsibility would the United States be justified in insisting that the will, or judgment, of the American people should be substituted for the will, or judgment, of the people of Great Britain? Japan was a member of the League and the World Court. It is also true that Great Britain was a member of the League and the World Court. Thus both nations, in disregard of the terms of the Covenant, sought a higher and more controlling covenant, and that was what was deemed national interests. (5)

Overall, Borah was an accomplished and respected senator, remaining popular despite his dissension. In 1921, he proposed a conference between the United States, Great Britain, and Japan to discuss ways to reduce naval expansion, and a naval limitation treaty resulted. As the Senate Foreign Relations Committee chairman since 1924, Borah was a dominant force in world affairs until an overwhelming Democratic majority became influential in 1933.

As one of the Senate's most eloquent and skilled orators, Borah was able to excite the American public's interest about a wide range of domestic and international issues. He roused the country when he denounced the gold standard as dishonest; called for a return to silver; suggested a reduction of worldwide armaments by 50 percent; and recommended canceling the debts owed to the United States from World War I. Later, he would support the Social Security Act and the Fair Labor Standards Act. Idaho especially loved its senator and in 1936, reelected him to his sixth consecutive term by 126,000 votes ("Borah," *American*).

He was popular with Pound as well. Although he was clearly disappointed that Borah dismissed him in Washington, the poet continued to write to him and grieved his death in a letter to the governor of Idaho: "If I who had met him only twice and known him before that by a series of brief letters, feel a personal loss, I can well imagine the feelings of those who had known him better" (appendix A).

Since the correspondence between Pound and Borah ended with the senator's death, we will never know how much longer Pound would have written to him. Shortly after Borah's death the Washington journalist Raymond Clapper complained that "there are no fighters on the progressive side—no men like T.R. . . . Borah was the last" (qtd. in Ashby 294). I would argue that both Borah and Pound were "fighters." What unfolds here is a correspondence that is less about what these two men held in common than about how strongly each adhered to his personal convictions.

*The Correspondence of Ezra Pound
and Senator William Borah*

1. POUND TO BORAH

TLS-2, Rapallo

27 November 1933

Senator Wm A.Borah

<Sir:> As an Idahoan, it wd. interest me to know whether your ignorance of the Bankhead bill[1] is real or pretended, and whether the american press boycotts mention of it from decent or indecent motives.

Is there a political game on, which requires that Stamp Scrip[2] remain unmentioned, or are all of you crooks and ALL OF YOU afraid to touch the dangerous subject of a real and PROVED remedy for a lot of trouble?

As to the unutterable Sprague.[3] He has sat in with the dirtiest crooks in Europe, the bastards that made the war, financed armaments in about-to-be hostile countries, and are still trying to sell more guns, and cook up more wars, by scares, bribery etc.

If he is not an accomplice he is simply too god damned dumb to have known what was going on around him.

In any case that is what the hired press calls an "expert economist."

Why the hell don't the schools give a little rudimentary education in economics, the history of economics, and in the use of language?

Al Smith[4] is a prize specimen of illiterate <, & fully demonstrates The—> effects of having no education.

The ubicty of Barney Baruch[5] wd. also make good copy if there were a contemporary NEWSPAPER anywhere in the country

Names of leading Tories, and of the 44 so called "economists"[6] said to be organizing in favor or restoring the great and universal stink of Harding/[7]Hoover/[8]Mellondom,[9] cd. also and with advantage be stuck up on a bill board, so 'z to know who has hired 'em to obscure the subject in their 44 separate beaneries.

cordially, for the first time in years,
Ezra Pound

GOD DAMN it all, can't you see that stamp Scrip permits MORE money WITHOUT inflation? No other system does except the C.H.Douglas[10] dividend.

1. The Bankhead-Pettengill bill was introduced into the Senate on 17 February 1933 by Senator John Hollis Bankhead of Alabama (1872–1946) and was co-sponsored by Representative Samuel Barrett Pettengill of Indiana (1886–1974). The bill called for a billion dollars in stamp scrip in an attempt to get currency circulating. As seen in letter 10, Pound thought the amount was excessive. In the *New English Weekly* issue of 26 October 1933, Pound writes that suggesting such a big sum was "the American Big Way—a bath, a swimming tank, where experiment had shown the efficiency of an injection" (31). Pound also argues that the bill would have passed if Bankhead had asked for a smaller amount. Bankhead was a supporter of the early New Deal, which probably left Pound unenthusiastic about him. In a letter to Mussolini he states that he did not "believe that he [Bankhead] understands things clearly" (qtd. in Heymann 318). Pound also expresses disappointment with him in canto 84 after he visited him in Washington but could not convince him of the validity of his ideas.

2. Silvio Gesell designed stamp scrip, or *Schwundgeld* (disappearing money), to combat inflation, but Pound saw it as a way to get money out of the "strangle-hold of the banking community" and to reduce taxes for the general population (qtd. in Heymann 71). Pound commented that such taxation "can only fall on persons who have, at the moment the tax falls due, money in their pockets worth 100 times the tax itself" (qtd. in Flory 70–71).

3. Oliver Mitchell Wentworth Sprague was a distinguished professor of economics and supported the international gold standard. Sprague served as an advisor and executive assistant to Secretary of the Treasury William H. Woodin in 1933 ("Sprague"). Pound considered it "an outrage" to call Sprague an expert ("As to" 3).

4. Alfred Smith, the governor of New York and president of the Empire State Building Corporation, battled Roosevelt for the presidential nomination in 1932

but lost. The two men were originally close, but Smith did not agree with Roosevelt's concern about lower-income citizens and later played an active part in the anti-Roosevelt American Liberty League ("Smith"). Nor was Smith interested in economic experimentation: "I am for gold dollars as against baloney dollars. I am for experience against experiment" (qtd. in Schlesinger, *Coming* 245).

5. Bernard Baruch was an American financier and an advisor to Roosevelt. Baruch opposed abandoning the gold standard (Schlesinger, *Coming* 201–2). Like Pound, he admired Borah, but Pound did not take to Baruch (McKenna 338). In addition to Baruch's conservative views on economics, Pound's anti-Semitism appeared to have affected his opinion of Baruch's political views. In one of Pound's radio broadcasts from Rome he said that Jews don't "care a hoot for law or for the American constitution" and that "every American boy that gets drowned owes it to Roosevelt and Baruch" (qtd. in Flory 154). Later, in St. Elizabeths Hospital, Pound paid someone to taste his food for him because he was afraid Baruch was trying to kill him. He said, "I can't understand why the Jews are after me" (qtd. in Flory 144).

6. The "44 so called 'economists'" is most likely a reference to something that occurred that very month. On 18 November 1933, the Chamber of Commerce demanded a return to the gold standard and a stop to experimentation. As a result, forty orthodox economists formed the Economists' National Committee on Monetary Policy and were led by E. W. Kemmerer of Princeton (Schlesinger, *Coming* 244).

7. Warren Gamaliel Harding (1865–1923) was the twenty-ninth president of the United States. Pound has grouped him with the "universal stink" of Hoover and Mellon because they represent the failed economic and political policies that led to the Great Depression. Pound viewed the election of Woodrow Wilson in 1912 and then the rise of the old guard Republicans under Harding, Coolidge, and Hoover as a dismal political landscape. Pound was given hope when the progressive movement was revived in 1931 by politicians such as William Borah and Bronson Cutting (Walkiewicz and Witemeyer 6).

8. Herbert Clark Hoover (1874–1964) was the thirty-first president of the United States.

9. One of America's richest businessmen, Andrew W. Mellon (1855–1937) had been the secretary of the treasury since the Hamilton administration. The government charged him with tax evasion, but he was exonerated (Schlesinger, *Crisis* 569–60).

10. After meeting Major Clifford Hugh Douglas in 1918, Pound became an advocate for his theories (Laughlin 153). Pound was a strong proponent of the dividend, a key component of Douglas's Social Credit theory. Douglas's answer to the problems of purchasing power was to construct a national dividend to which all citizens, except the very wealthy, were entitled (Burns 21).

2. BORAH TO POUND

TLS-1, [Washington]

3 January 1934
E. Pound,
Rapallo, via Marsala 12–5,
Italy.

My dear Mr. Pound:

"As an Idahoan" I suggest that you come back to Idaho and to the United States. It isn't fair to give us so much "hell" at so great a distance. I can talk better than I can write. So drop in when you get home and see me.

> Very sincerely,
> William E. Borah

3. POUND TO BORAH

TL-4, [Rapallo]

15 January 1934

My Dear Senator

"Honest", you dont know when you're well off. If my ole man hadn't cleared out of Hailey[1] in 1888, they'd have made him territorial delegate. And you know how long it takes to get a NEW idea into an Idaho head! He wd. nacherly have riz when the state became, and heaven knows how long it wd. have taken other people to become senior committee men. Don' you talk to me about Geography. When you think of the foreign countryies you have AUTHORITY'D, without knowing whether they were in Europe Asia or Afrikaaa!!!

However, I appreciate the ibvitation. If there is anything that don't interest me, it is conversation.

Seriously. There are a number of S/O/B whom we wd. both like to see buried. There were 44 gold swine drawing professorial pay.

Might remember that yr/ old friend (?) Kitson[2] wrote me in Dec. "The two best were fired for using my first book as a text book". (I.E. two best economics professors in the U.S.)

Bank de France running Mitnui,[3] to sell guns to Russia.etc. Sprague the cronies of those really putrid devils.

Congressional record might as well be a secret document, as far as getting news of Bankhead Pettengill bill to the peePul!!

The arsenic I am offering is the following brief questionnaire. NO MAN TO BE RANKED AS AN ECONOMIC EXPERT till he has answered the three questions (not even by the Noo Yok Hearld, or Times, or the Kreuger-boosting Sat. Eve. Post.[4])

I. What is an auxilliary currency?

II. When money is rented, who ought to pay the rent, the man who has the money when the rent falls due, or some bloke who HASN'T?

III. What is the result of every factory, every industry, under the present system, creating prices faster than it emits the power to buy??[5]

Frank D. is THE great artist of carom shot.... and it is possible in state of pubk/ iGGURREnce to turn out a new brand of hooey each week. quite honestly and with a decent objective.

Still. The worst reactionaries aren't dead YET.

Dont you worry about a few American's being starved in Europe (I am taking it light heartedly because I think it better that 120 million shd/ be looked after FIRST). But that triple skink Wilson[6] wd/ have saved time if he had got his European news from Americans in Europe rather than from Missouri.[7]

And as fer the last whitehouse sofa Mr H.

"I am sorry, Mr H." said the jedge "that this hwe been brought as a civil and not as a criminal action!"[8]

Country needs a few Ambassadors (informal and NOT subject to appointment by men like Hoover and Harding.) Also a news service wdnt do any harm.

There isn't a contemporary newspaper in the U.S.

A hardboild newspaper ex manager in N.Y.[9] was very keen on my starting one. He suggested gettin money from Woodin,[10] Wiggin[11] and Barney Baruch!!

Only the telegraph worked quicker than the postal service... so his letter was a REAL treat.

Thank god THAT WAS OF SERVING ONES COUNTRY IS less promising than it was.

What has become of Senator Bankhead? Did he see his "shadder" on the ground after he brought in that exuberant bill and putt fer his burrow?

Absolootly THE forgotten man!

Come on, be decent, if the govt. is blowing 40 billion, pay out 50 million in stamp scrip. What the HELL is the use trying to hide the fact that it works. Woergl[12] demonstration. WORKED.

yours cordially

1. Hailey, Idaho, is Pound's birthplace.
2. Arthur Kitson was an inventor, engineer, and author of *The Bankers' Conspiracy*. His theories greatly influenced Pound (Wilhelm 56).

3. Pound frequently attacked the partnerships of banks and munitions companies. The Japanese bank Mitsui supported the Taiping Company's munitions sales to Russia. Both Mitsui and Taiping profited immensely, similar to how J. P. Moran and Co. profited from supplying war goods to the Allied powers (Roberts 195–96).

4. Ivar Kreuger was a Swedish financier who killed himself on 12 March 1932 and whose death, in addition to the suicide of George Eastman, prompted people to wonder about the stress with which these financiers lived. Kreuger had been interviewed with great adoration for the *Saturday Evening Post*. However, after his death he and other financiers were revealed as swindlers (Schlesinger, *Crisis* 254). In the 10 January 1935 issue of the *New English Weekly* Pound writes, "no member of the public should ever be allowed to forget that the 'Saturday Evening Post,' one of the few American publications bloated enough to be on sale on almost every European bookstall, told its million readers that Krueger was 'more than a financial titan'" and that "there are some unforgivable sins" (270).

5. On 22 March 1934, Borah remarked, "We know the purchasing power of the people is at a very low level, perhaps the lowest in history, and shall we reduce acreage, destroy food, thus compelling less and less consumption because purchasing power is not there to take care of the higher prices?" He went on to implore, "We must restore purchasing power" and "should seek to establish a monetary system which will give the peoples of the world a system commensurate with their needs" ("Radio" 1–4). Pound would add in *New Democracy* on 15 May 1934 that "THE NEXT AND ONLY HONEST move is to distribute it [purchasing power] IMPARTIALLY per capita" ("Ahead" 5).

6. Woodrow Wilson was president of the United States from 1913 to 1921. Pound disliked Wilson for a variety of reasons, the chief being that he brought the United States into World War I. Pound blamed the 1913 Federal Reserve Act for the problems he saw in the banking system. In a 1951 letter Pound writes, "Federal Reserve act, signed by Woodie Wilson the damned, Dec 23, 1913, so that the bankers wd/ lose nothing by THAT war" (qtd. in Tryphonopoulos and Surette 69). In 1918, also under the Wilson administration, Congress adopted the Passport Control Act, which was extended into peacetime. Pound became a strong opponent of passports and denounced them continually in his letters and articles. In a letter to Senator Bronson Cutting, Pound writes, "Dem/ party, cd. be reminded of Wilson's push for bureaucracy and the passport infamies" (qtd. in Walkiewicz and Witemeyer 61).

7. This is most likely a reference to Champ Clark (1850–1921) of Missouri, who served in the House of Representatives from 1893 to 1895 and from 1897 to 1921. He was Speaker of the House during 1911–19 and was also a member of the Foreign Affairs Committee (Walkiewicz and Witemeyer 119).

8. Pound is referring to a 1905 lawsuit in London in which an English min-

ing company (which had employed Herbert Hoover as an engineer) was deemed to have unethically obtained property in China. Pound's paraphrase is not an accurate representation of events, but he repeats himself many other times, such as in canto 97 (Walkiewicz and Witemeyer 64).

9. This is possibly a reference to the editor Henry Lewis Mencken (1880–1956), who was one of Roosevelt's greatest critics (Schlesinger, *Coming* 565).

10. William H. Woodin (1868–1934) was secretary of state for a short time in 1933. He was also the president of the American Car and Foundry Company and gave money to Roosevelt's campaign (Schlesinger, *Crisis* 280).

11. Albert H. Wiggin of Chase Bank was one of New York's great bankers. He said that there would be "times that are prosperous and times that are not prosperous" and that "there is no commission or any brain in the world that can prevent it" (qtd. in Schlesinger, *Crisis* 178).

12. A form of stamp scrip was put into circulation in the village of Wörgl until the Austrian government learned of the experiment and ousted the mayor, whom Pound would later visit (Laughlin 159). Pound writes about the experiment in canto 74: "the state need not borrow / as was shown by the mayor of Worgl / who had a milk route / and whose wife sold shirts and short breeches." Pound commented in the 26 October 1933 issue of the *New English Weekly* that "with the example of Woergl eminently successful, a series of American towns issued stamp-script with no determined date for affixing the stamps, thus diminishing the urge to spend, and permitting collusion between spender and receiver for omitting the stamps altogether. Nevertheless, so useful is auxiliary coinage . . . that even this botched method was beneficial" (31).

4. POUND TO BORAH

TL-2, [Rapallo]

24 March 1934
Senator W.E.Borah

My Dear Senator

    I have at last got hold of the Congressional Record for Jan. 27 with Senator Cutting's speech.[1] That was spoken like a man and an honest one.

    It is all very well for you to suggest that I could curse more effectively if I were in Idaho or Washington. I am not sure of it. If I knew any was of getting Farley[2] out of the District of Columbia or preventing people with no more intelligence than HULL[3] from being appointed to positions demanding at least the barins of street car conductor, I might risk the boat fare.

    Dont you honestly think there is some way of eliminating cowards from controll of what wits the naton nation possesses?

    I mean WHAT is the use of accepting men as "economic authorities" when they will NOT stand up to simple questions?

    I dare say after years in office you get used to being surrounded by crooks and idiots, but surely you must be fed up.

    Hasn't any in the Senate got the guts to follow up Cutting's remarks?

    Why shouldn't the administration AND the "economists" be forced to answer at least one of
[line(s) missing]

    What is the result of every factory, every industry creating prices faster than it emits the power to buy?

    Are you going to lie down and let the N.Y. TIMES!!!! push up a new "economist once in every three weeks" (Sprague!!!, and now WARREN!!!)[4]

    Is the nations purchasing power to be distributed honestly and impartially to the citizens AS SUCH or eternally hoahed to different gangs. Last year it was Gene Myer's[5] philanthropists/ Swope's[6] gang was ready to take on etc..

When meney is rented who ought to pay the rent, the man who has the money when the rent falls due, or some bloke who hasn't?

In the interim can you supply we with the names of six senators who have traces of intelligence and a little moral or intellectual courage? I mean blokes that wont hide their heard under the covers whenever the meet a question.

cordially yours

1. Senator Bronson Cutting (1888–1935) was a progressive Republican from New Mexico with whom Pound corresponded. The *Congressional Record* for 27 January records a speech in which he discussed "the purchasing power of the masses of the people" and remarked, "The place we want credit is in the hands of the consumer. I do not think it necessary to argue that point at this time in the history of the United States. Three or four years ago people thought you were crazy when you talked about equating the purchasing power of the country with the productive power. Now everybody recognizes that, so far as speech is concerned. We talk about purchasing power, but we take little action about it" (*Cong. Rec.* 1476).

2. James A. Farley was postmaster general under Roosevelt and was also a member of an American delegation to the International Monetary and Economic Conference. At the time Pound wrote this letter, Farley was being criticized for canceling air-mail contracts. After the Army Air Corps had to step in to deliver the mail, several pilots died. The historian Arthur Schlesinger notes that Farley actually had little to do with the decision to cancel the contracts (*Coming* 453). Farley had little faith in Borah's campaign abilities and noted that he was merely a "quarter-mile runner" (qtd. in Leuchtenburg 105). In the *New English Weekly* Pound commented on 10 January 1935 that Farley was helpful in ensuring that Roosevelt was "in touch with the old organisation," whom he believed was "a very corrupt but powerful set of thieves and barrators" ("American Notes" 270). Although Pound did not like Farley, he visited Pound at St. Elizabeths (Heymann 193).

3. A Former congressman and senator, Secretary of State Cordell Hull (1871–1955) advocated passage of the Reciprocal Trade Agreements Act, which had been criticized by Borah as unconstitutional (Schlesinger, *Coming* 255). Perhaps because of Hull's indifference to arguments over monetary standards (Schlesinger, *Coming* 253), Pound thought him a "peril to the nation" ("American Notes," 10 Jan 1935: 270). Toward the end of 1935, Hull would favor the

suspension of supplies to Italy and thus deny the country war materials (Hardie 111).

4. A professor of farm management at Cornell, George F. Warren (1874–1938) advised Roosevelt about the depression. Warren believed that the general price theory was contingent on the price of gold (Schlesinger, *Coming* 234).

5. A member of the Federal Reserve Board, which controlled the supply of credit in the United States, Eugene Meyer was not favored by Pound (Walkiewicz and Witemeyer 57). Meyer was also chairman of the Reconstruction Finance Corporation, an agency for cooperation between government and business. In the spring of 1934 Meyer declared that he did not think intellectuals should advise the government (Schlesinger, *Coming* 425, 73).

6. An executive at General Electric, Gerald Swope thought that national economics could be improved with trade associations (Schlesinger, *Coming* 89).

5. POUND TO BORAH

TLS-1, Rapallo

16 April 1934
W.E.Borah U.S.Senate

Dear Senator

Cant remember the Trib.[1] ever having spoken well of you BEFORE, but instead of printing what you SAID they give this unintelligible whoop. O.K. as far as it goes.

Any way to get copy of speech?[2] In senate or outside?

I don't trust the Trib. ten feet. Though they did print a two col/ head last week re Italy in which I pointed out that capitalism was a syphilis that rotted the inmost processes of the mind. <Hope [?] don't see it. / better he shouldn't.>

They have a biasd/ stick this a/m/ saying Italy cuts govt. pay. BUT NOT saying that at same time RENTS (all every and any) go down Io% and so do food stuffs) also pay cuts start ABOVE 500 lire per month.

The stinking Frogs, are 30 years behind Italy. They cut pay, but NOT rents and food cost.

Italy not Douglasite YET/ but these successive Io% cuts on rent, are just as useful to the average man as a Doug dividend.

Encl a little English Lucidity, not from a poET.

yrs   E.P.

<I WONDER begod, did you get around to SAYING anything real in that speech. And between ourselves, does F.D. UNDERSTAND anything? or it it all good humour and water<-melons?>

1. This is a reference to the *International Herald Tribune*.
2. Pound is most likely referring to Borah's speech of 22 March 1934, in which the senator made a variety of comments about two of Pound's favorite ideas, distribution and purchasing power. Borah expressed concern with the current system for distributing food and clothing and believed, therefore, there was not a problem with overproduction.

6. POUND TO CUTTING [AND BORAH]

TL-1, [Rapallo]

22 April [1934]

My Dear Senator

HOW the hell can honest men stay on Industrial Advisory Board without pay?[1]

I mean how the hell can the one presumably intelligent man (who aint rich) stick on it with the bloated ploots. unless he gets his hotel bill.

As an opposition member... might be a tactful constructive act to suggest that W.E.Woodward[2] get a salary.

I dont spose they've got any other members with two louse's worth of sense.

EF th KENTRY iz to use men's WORK and all their workin time, it ought to pay 'em.

    1. W. E. Woodward informed Pound that members of the Industrial Advisory Board were not paid (Walkiewicz and Witemeyer 124). The board was one of the three parts of the National Recovery Administration, which included industry, labor, and consumers (Schlesinger, *Coming* 128).

    2. Not only did he serve on Roosevelt's Business Advisory Council but William E. Woodward was also a historian and the author of such books as *A New American History* and *George Washington, the Image and the Man*. After reading the latter, Pound started writing to him in 1933 and began what would be a mutual correspondence and friendship (Wilhelm 77–81).

7. POUND TO BORAH

TLS-2, Rapallo

8 May 1934
Senator W.E.Borah

My Dear Senator

I was glad to see yr/ suggestion that the repub/ party shd/ delouse and find a leader. The Trib. suggested that you meant Mr H. wdnt. do. This a/m/. <one said> Herbie Hoover iz reported as saying he don't expect to be candidate in whenever. I havent the bastards address but shd. be glad if you wd. communicate my opinion i/e/ tell that fat cheater of chinamen[1] that the only things about him that cd. run are his nose or his hemeroids.

I don't see the Lamont[2] and Whitney[3] nurseries producing a winner? You have yourself boxed the compass, just a bit. I don't see you carrying the country UNLESS you can use the next three years (two years) in DEFINING an enlightened econ. policy.

I mean, confound you, you wd. have to be MORE DEFINITE than F.D.R. who has gone further than you have, and has defined more than you have. And has shown up the god damd scoundrels very neatly in pubing/ that list of N.Y.banks who are trying to push off a lot of perfectly useless metal (happens to be silver) on the usual goAT, the peepul.[4]

I suppose Mellon is too downy a bird to finish in jail.

But a little republican ZEAL about getting Wiggin, Insull[5] and the whole god damn lot of 'em jugged, wd. go strong with the electorate.

ALSO why not start on reform of the Universities. The jig is damn well UP. Can't go on suppressing history, of the U.S.A. OF economics etc. forever. Mostly been done on REPUBLIC endowments.

If YOU don't get to THAT first F.D. will be thaaar nice and ahead of you settin' pretty.

Also the Carnegie Peace fund scandal,[6] that wd. come better from repub/ party than from the other side. <as Butler[7] is one of the lights of republican poopery>

I dont blame YOU for what the garbage party has been. I know from my grandfather's life, all about the theory of "FROM WITHIN the party".

He kept that terd Blaine[8] out of the White House, but it busted him. BUT hang it all, you GOT to move if you mean anything serious.

<truly yrs>[?]

E. Pound

1. Pound refers to Hoover as a "cheater of chinamen" because some writers accused him of cheating the Chinese government as well as oppressing Chinese labor in the United States when he took over Kaiping mines in China for a British firm in which he held a substantial interest (Roberts 197). Arthur Schlesinger argues that such a reputation partially explains why Hoover's name became a derogatory prefix, as in "Hooverville" (*Crisis* 245).

2. Thomas W. Lamont (1870–1948), of the J. P. Morgan and Company banking firm, was grilled during the Pecora Committee investigation of Wall Street when he took the stand with George Whitney and Richard Whitney in the spring of 1933 (Schlesinger, *Coming* 434–35). Lamont also appears in canto 19 as "Tommy Baymont" (Terrell 79).

3. George Whitney worked at J. P. Morgan and Company. Richard Whitney was the president of the New York Stock Exchange and opposed regulation of the industry (Schlesinger, *Coming* 461). He was convicted of trading irregularities and sent to prison. During his testimony before the Pecora Committee, George Whitney observed, "It is hard to answer why we did things. It is even harder to say why we didn't" (qtd. in Schlesinger, *Coming* 438).

4. Borah's interest in banking is evident in his speeches. On 4 July 1934, he proclaimed, "If permitted to act under general just and equal laws, with an adequate monetary system and an adequate banking system, protected from the exactions of monopoly, free also from the restraint and dictation of bureaucracy, the people will win this war against depression" (17).

5. Samuel Insull (1859–1938) helped monopolize Chicago Edison and then founded the Insull utility group. After being hit by the depression, he attempted to save his estate with loans. He was unable to pay back his debts, became vilified in the eyes of the public, and eventually fled to Europe after being acquitted of embezzlement, larceny, and mail fraud charges (Bondi 129–31).

6. The Carnegie Endowment for International Peace was established in 1910. In the 25 July 1935 issue of the *New English Weekly* Pound claims that "pacifists who refuse to investigate the economic causes of war make common cause with

the gun sellers. I sincerely hope Congressman Tinkham will keep on with his agitation for the investigation of endowments, in particular re the use of funds by the Carnegie Endowment for Peace" ("History and Ignorance" 287). In the *New Democracy* issue of 1 December 1935, Pound alleges that one reason for war is that banks make money from collecting interest on loans made to foreign countries engaged in war. Pound maintains that "with their vast organization for tabulation and 'research' the Carnegie Peace blokes MIGHT have found this out years ago. When the public finds it out there will be less call for Peace Organizations" (120).

7. Nicholas Murray Butler (1862–1947) was the president of Columbia University (1901–45) and head of the Carnegie Foundation for International Peace (1925–45). Pound did not think Butler was doing a good job (Walkiewicz and Witemeyer 127). He wrote a letter to Butler with Albert von Mensdorff-Pouilly-Dietrichstein, an agent for the Carnegie Endowment for Peace, but Butler wrote a token reply that angered Pound (Wilhelm 31).

8. James Gillespie Blaine (1830–93) was nominated for president in 1884, but Grover Cleveland won the election ("Blaine").

8. POUND TO BORAH

TLS-2, Rapallo

15 May 1934
W.E.Borah. U.S.Senate

My Dear Senator:

Thanks very much for copy of yr/ radio speech. Bravo, as far as it goes. I.E. It is all in last paragraph on p. I. and final sentence on p. 5.

NOW what hindereth thee to be baptised? WHY the hell not mention the two inventions that make distribution possible?

Douglas' dividends. vide "New Democracy," or Stamp Scrip.

I enclose the last news which appeared in the "Lavoro"[1] of Genoa. The free press (i;e; that hog tied by Deterding,[2] de Wendel,[3] and the murderers' league) has naturally not reported the move.

Are you and senator Cutting on speakin' terms, and if not WHY not?

I am sending the copy of yr/ speech up to London, but can't be sure it will be quoted. ANYHOW, god dman it, our HOME market matters, and all the foreign trade isn't worth half a hoot in comparison. Red herring, and has served the financiers, as smoke screen to such extent, that it cd. be left out of all pubk/ discussion for ten years.

WHAT about a campaign for reform of university teaching? Why not look for'rad a bit, and see that the yearly crop of mis-educated college boys is a yearly rivet in grandfather's neck?

Not disappointed about Andy/ as I always thought he was too downy to die in jail.

BUT WHEN do we start enquiring into Nic Butler? AND the sources of income of the purrfessers of economic damn lying, cornfed in the financial pocket boroughs?

LACK of purchasing power is NOT static.

Every factory, every industry, under the preset shitten and snotten system <u>produces prices FASTER than it emits the power to buy.</u>

THAT is what you got to tell 'em on the raido. Go to it Bruvver B.

yrz

E. Pound

1. The *Lavoro* (meaning "labor" in English) was an Italian newspaper. Pound sent a small clipping to Borah along with his letter. The article is entitled "Singolare Progetto Perfavorire la Rinascita Economica del Principato di Monaco" and is about the Union of Commerce and Industry of Monaco adopting a plan, similar to stamp scrip, to promote the economic revival of currency ("Singolare" 9).

2. Sir Henry Deterding was director-general of the Royal Dutch Petroleum Company, which later merged with Shell Oil. He was part of a group of businessmen who chastised Borah for his amicable relationships with Russian politicians and diplomats (McKenna 297).

3. François de Wendel was the son of the president of the French Comité des Forges, which was responsible for the majority of munitions sales prior to and following World War I (Wilhelm 101). Besides being a director of the Bank of France, he was also said to have control over *Le Temps, Le Journal des débats,* and *Echo de Paris* (Walkiewicz and Witemeyer 109). Pound considered him an evil force and in the 15 May 1934 issue of *New Democracy* wrote that Europe was "groaning under De Wendel" (5). In canto 38, he claimed that the war made money for de Wendel's papers.

9. BORAH TO POUND

TLS-1, Washington

21 May 1934
E. Pound,
Rapallo, via Marsala 12-5,
Italy.

My dear friend Pound:

   Delighted to have your letter. I feel I am occasionally catching up to you.

   I am sending you a copy of a speech of mine lately made,[1] but I dread the comments which you will make. However, it may be helpful to do so.

   When are you returning to Idaho?

Very sincerely,
William E. Borah

   1. This is most likely a reference to a speech made four days prior on 17 May 1934. Borah spoke about the Constitution and against fascism.

10. POUND TO BORAH

TL-6, [Rapallo]

2 June 1934

NOW. Have ypu, CONFOUND it, HAVE you read my ABC of Economics?

Gesell[1] had one stoke of genius. Mere payment of govt. expenses by fiat money would mean inflation, i;e; everybody having to pay more money for whiskey and cigars and boots.

BUT the moment the idea of scrip with a monthly stamp on it was discovered, the way to justice was clear.

[line(s) missing]

credit are those who perform services so necessary that the state pays the bill.

As you were at the supper to Douglas, I suppose you see the New English Weekly and New Democracy. Whatever I write in those papers is probably stated with more care than what I pour into the morning's private letters. 5 reasons for talking stamp scrip appear in N.E.W. May 31.[2]

In case of Stamp Scrip the TAX falls <u>on the</u> money itself (I mean if you still have an idee fixe re/ TAX. and want to describe the monthly stamp as tax.)

Bankhead went off half cocked in Feb. last year. Billion!! me YA RRSE!!! 30 million wd/ have been nearer the mark AUXILLIARY CURRENCY.

The heckers (including all England and the readers of Beaver/Rothers[3] swill) DONT KNOW that France started using auxilliary currency in 1919/ issued by chambers of commerce.

The opponents of Stamp scrip talk as if anyone expected it to constitute the WHOLE currency.

[line(s) missing]

re/ all and any public works campaigns. ////:::::

IT IS INFAMY for the state to get into debt to individuals by the very act of creating real wealth.

This they obviously do by borrowing. BUT WOULD NOT DO by paying for all pubk/ works in stamp scrip.

Did I say that last year I wrote a book "Jefferson and/or Mussolini" that NO one will print. (4 books in Eng/ one in U.S. pubd/ last year/ 4 Eng/ 2 for U.S. contracted for this year. so it is not objection to ME but to the matter of the book.)

Also my refs/ to Jefferson and VanBuren in coming CANTOS.

T.Jeff/ on debt. etc.

W.E.Woodward wrote a VERY stong recommendation of the Jeff/ Muss mss/ a few weeks ago but even that wont carry it into print. My GORRRD we need university reform. We need to root out the snotty profs and Spragues who have been concealing history.

Van Buren autobiography unprinted from 1861 till 1920!!!

(Cantos XXXI/XLI are due for publication in N.Y. and
[line(s) missing]

editrss wd/ fall overherself sending you copies if you'd request 'em by post card. The ole gal is mad as hell cause I wont write about dasies and dicky birds and li'l bybies a suckin at mama.

Anyhow, they summarize some of the country's glory/ and IF intellgible should assist the reform of the party.

As Frankie' seems to have avoided C.H.D. (<being> represented among the just and enquiring only by Berle[4]) I dare say Cutting's supper part[5] represents ALL the mental life of the country.

I take it that as soon as Gene Myers theves got putt of the Fed Cont. Board// The Swope gang tried to steal the country and failed almost by accident.

(allus willin to learn.)

At any rate Frank is too muzzy to have any more power handed him/ so cheeuhs fer the Constitution, long may it wave and SOON may it cease to waver.

BUT there hadnt orter BE any god damn taxes, save the tax ON money itself and possibly a poll tax of one dollar simply to prove technically and academicly that the stamp scrip is legal tender.

I was glad to see the account of Cutting's supper party, as I had [line(s) missing]

anythime you think there wd. be any REAL USE in havin' me snarlin' round trying to hammer a little economic sense into yr/ colleagues.

Whether I wd/ be any more use on the spot, than pluggin away in New Eng. Weekly/ New Dem/ and wherever else I am let loose, I dunno.

There seem to have been more Dems/ that Reps/ at the supper. The last bloke that had a drink with the Rep/ white hope Teethadore Jr/[6] sez T.R. is a prime and perfect specimen of moron/ so the hope of dynastic analogy dont seem heavy. I mean the stock exchange seems to be looking for another simple minded Gamaliel.[7] to serve as shop front for pork.

Scrip seems to me the WAY. I mean the next step, as Douglas' plan requires human intellegence to puttt into into practice, and gorrnoze human intelligence is lacking in govt circles. ESPECIALLY in pore bloody england.

Vickers/[8] Thysson/[9] Mitsui/ Schneider/[10] Bank of France.

An econ/ system that makes it more profitable to sell guns in the hope of mass murder, than to distribute food and clothing is shit over shit to eternity, and its supporters deserve no more mercy than the late Russian half wit Nicholas/ in fact as a /ass Nich Butler isn't half a cut above Nic Romanoff.[11] (speaking a syzogy and metrical ornament).

As politics/ couldn't one start with the aphorisms (rather Frankie's trick) and gradually lead to new Econ/ by that route.

[line(s) missing]

gets assent from every honest man, long before he can understand the MEANS to prevent the infamy.

The reason why VanBuren's speech (vide Canto 37[12]) had to be so vague was that TAX problem hadn't been cleared.

Thinking over yr/ speech, I reckon you did a good job of CONSTRUCTION nailing tarrif onto TAX.

The idea isn't new; but the nail was needed. And a lot of popular education, broadcast etc/ along that line would be very useful.

Re: all F/D/'s yawp. IF the issue can be kept clear, IF it is constantly YELLED: in the form: WHY distribute purchasing power to special interests (via subsidies etc) INSTEAD of impartially to citizens PER CAPITA.

I dont see that F/D/ and his wobbler HAVE any POSSIBLE answer. (vide New Democracy for May 15th. P. 5 col.3. over distinguished signature (vide infra).¹³

nuff fer one senator fer one day.

Cordially

1. Silvio Gesell designed the notion of stamp scrip.

2. In the 31 May 1934 issue of the *New English Weekly,* Pound lists the five reasons: it "terrifies" the people who "make" war; it is a form of currency that cannot be hoarded; the tax falls on the currency itself (and therefore never on anyone who cannot pay it); it is avoided by the "filth" of society (and therefore is proof that honest people should examine it); and it is "an infinite gain to humanity" ("Letter" 167).

3. Baron Max Aitken Beaverbrook (1879–1964) owned such papers as the *London Daily Express* and the *London Evening Standard* ("Beaverbrook"). Viscount Rothermere (Harold Sidney Harmsworth) (1868–1940) co-owned the *Daily Mail* and the *Evening News,* among others (Walkiewicz and Witemeyer 109).

4. Adolf Augustus Berle Jr. (1895–1971) was a professor at Columbia Law School, a member of the Brain Trust, and an advisor to Roosevelt for many years (Schlesinger, *Crisis* 399; *Coming* 240).

5. Senator Bronson Cutting writes to Pound that Borah was one of the "open-minded" senators he invited to a dinner party he was having for C. H. Douglas (qtd. in Walkiewicz and Witemeyer 128).

6. The nickname "Teethadore" is for Theodore Roosevelt Jr. (1887–1944). He was an active Republican who devoted his time to the American Liberty League after the Democrats came to power (Walkiewicz and Witemeyer 122–27). Borah criticized the league because he thought its members were hypocritical (Schlesinger, *Coming* 489).

7. This is a reference to Warren Gamaliel Harding.

8. The Vickers family was the British co-owner of Vickers-Armstrong, one of Britain's largest armaments makers, known as "Ackers" in the cantos: "And Ackers made a large profit and imported gold into England. Thus increasing gold imports" (canto 38). Pound often wondered how many wars had been started just to sell munitions (Walkiewicz and Witemeyer 109).

9. Founded in 1891, Thyssen supplied Germany with steel in both world wars (Sawinski and Mason 506).

10. Schneider was a munitions industrialist company (Wilhelm 98).

11. Nicholas II (Nicholas Romanov) was the last czar of Russia.

12. In canto 37, Pound attempts to rehistoricize President Martin Van Bu-

ren as a hero of the people because he did not want the U.S. Treasury to fall into private hands.

13. In the 15 May 1934 issue of *New Democracy,* Pound writes that it is one thing for Roosevelt to talk about purchasing power; it is another to decide "TO WHOM shall the gov't distribute its purchasing power" ("Ahead" 5).

11. POUND TO BORAH

TLS-3, Rapallo

7 June 1934
Senator WE Borah

My Dear Senator

I have just had a seven page letter from W.E.Woodward complaining that Douglas (C.H.) didn't answer his question ETC.

The whole of W.E.W's muddle arising from his not having grasped the possibility of a FIXED price, let alone of "compensated or adjusted or just "price.

If a man as intelligent as Woodward, as near to the works, hasn't SEEN that yet, there must be "countless millions" needing primary instruction.

You got over the POINT re/ distribution in the radio talk you sent me.[1] Is there any reason why you or Senator Cutting shdn't. go on the air with the simple facts re/ possibility of FIXING prices (of necessities, say, food stuffs (bacic) and even certain qualities of well made textiles TO THE CONSUMER.

You have fixed prices TO THE PRODUCER on wheat etc in the U.S.A.

But the bloody bastardly suppression and distortion, and fundamentally indifferent and unintelligent lack of interest in Italian news has wasted peoples' time and they do not REALIZE that here we have the price of meat, bread etc. posted up on the walls <of market. etc> and people do NOT have to pay more.

I suggest the utility of the following course of argument. <on radio.>

I. The existence of anything proves that it is POSSIBLE (i;e; <that> it is possible for it to exist)

II. Prices TO THE CONSUMER were <in various countries.> fixed during and after the war. They are now FIXED by decree in Italy. This don't prove that we <americans> ought to change the form of American govt. and turn fascist. It proves that fascism DOES certain things, and if the things it DOES are more intelligent that what the U.S.Govt. is now doing, the U.S.Govt. ought to LEARN.[2]

III. The value of money is WHAT it will BUY. Money is worth what you can GET for it.

A system of inflation or deflation or any other damn wangle that TAKES no count of WHAT the money will buy, is a hoax.

IV. Quite obviously DOUGLAS' economics will NOT WORK if you omit one of the cheif FACTORS. ANY more than a tripod will stand up if you remove one of its legs.

V. FIXED price is one of Doug's MAIN factors. IT is a special KIND of fixed price; based on JUSTICE, that is to say it is based on what the COMMODITY REALLY COSTS to the nation.

The system for computing this cost is no more complicated that the system of computing costs NOW used in any trust or manufacturing company.

VI. All <so called> arguments against Douglas' which leave out the FIXED (just) price, are NOT arguments against <Dougl but against> the arguer's own muddle and miscomprehension.

I am sending carbon of this to Senator Cutting. IF there is any -POSSIBLE obscurity in the above statement I wd/ be grateful to have it pointed out.

cordially
E. Pound

I'll send details re/ Italian price system if wanted. Prices of some things settled by local authorities/ taking count of local conditions/ reshipments etc. of food stuffs etc.

Obviously the reductions of RENTS here act pretty much as a DIVIDEND. Just as Muss' grain policy, reduced railway fares, drainage etc. ACT as MATERIAL DIVIDENDS.

The god damn british (including Doug's informal staff, have been cornfed on British press lies etc. a nd are NOT UP TO DATE in understanding of Italy and what gets done here. (they are quick as mice to yell about what AINT.

1. See letter 9.

2. Here, and in many other passages, Pound tries to barter fascism. Borah, however, will later publicly dismiss it in his speeches. On 6 May 1937, Borah will assert that "democracy is worth saving, worth fighting for" and that "no one can be a loyal American citizen who advocates or believes in fascism" ("Fascism" 4). On 23 June 1937, Borah is harsher, announcing that those who buy into fascism are "traitors" and that those who say "that they can be loyal to fascism and naziism and still be true Americans" are wrong. He will add, "Everyone must know that that cannot be true, and it cannot be thought to be true by any man possessed of intellectual integrity" ("Fascism" 2).

12. POUND TO BORAH

TL-3, Rapallo

7 July 1934
W.E. Borah Esq

My Dear Senator

From report in yesterday's Paris "Trib" you seem to have got over ANOTHER one. But mere absence of bugocracy wont do the trick. The advantage of consumer credit, dividends, credit-controll IS that it eliminates bugocracy. is simple and clean, whereas to controll production you have to have two controllers for every producer.

Is Frankie run (oh well, I spose not WHOLLY) by jews? merely left another choosich dictator behind when he went sailin'.

Baruch is acc/ last printed report said to have boasted he controlled, oh hell, I have lost it but it was about 230 out of 260 american gun firms, or more prob. was in Europe to sell for that numner back in I9I5 or thereabouts, and some <Morgenthau[1]> said to have had a lot of gun shares. (German report and treatable with reserve, as I believe Morg/ <ole ambas/ to Turkey> finally convinced Wilson (damn him) that Germany was a hostile power.

Hell, you have got a tough row to hoe if you are going to clean the republican party. As I may have written, my grand dad kept <helped keep> Blaine OUT, but it cost him the remainder of his career. I spose Grover was worth it at the time.

I think Mussolini wd. be the last man to want Italian fascism in America, perfectly aware at least that fascist dialect wd. be useless there. BUT I doubt if you will find any man in power with greater care for the public good, I mean OF the people, or pushing harder to get it DE FACTO by whatever verbal formula, (never going so fast as to cut himself off from the general comprehension).

The price cust and rent cuts here, have temporary effect of DIVI-

DEND, in fact they have more than that, the do constitute a dividend for everyone who is getting ANY money at all. rent cut 12% (and that I think is the third time in five or six years. Have been at least three, I forget the dates.) Also the advertised <govt.> PAY cuts, affected only salaries ABOVE a certain figure.

Got more sense than F.D's crowd.

Also capable of THINKING about my somewhat startling statement <u>If money is considered as certificate of work done, taxation is unnecessary.</u>

A god damn outrage that all (or practically all) new purchasin power shd/ come into existence as DEBT.

Fr/ Xtz ache get THAT into the electorate. You'll get a bloody fine muniment even if you dont get into the Casa Blanca.

Personally I prefer a bloke like Mussolini who really has prevented war; and more than once, to a soapy faced son of a bitch like Nic Butler who talks about pecae, and NEVER looks at (or never speaks of) the economic causes of war.

cordially yrs

1. Henry Morgenthau Sr. (1856–1946) was a businessman, a powerful Democrat, and the ambassador to Turkey during the Wilson administration (Schlesinger, *Coming* 243).

13. POUND TO BORAH

TL-2, [Rapallo]

[1934]

All Right Bruvver//

"To hell with bureaucracy". IF you can get nominated with an ISSUE, that will be quite nice. And to get nominated, you've got to convince bruvver Lamont and co/ that they will damn well get licked if they put up any more Hoovers or shit or that kind.

Also as Arthur Griffiths[1] said to me "Cant move 'em with a COLD thing like economics."

Will you take off 20 minutes and conisder "NO TAXES" as a campaign slogan. And will you think for 20 minutes about HOW you can keep that promise.?

Single tax/ tax on LAND is hooey/ or rather it is Fulton's steam boat/ WAS once an idea.

IF MONEY is considered as certificate of work done, taxes are no longer necessary. (If you dont understand think, god damn it I will explain.) All govt. papyments shd/ be made in stamp scrip (stamp 1% to be affixed first of every month.)

That is, if you like a tax on money. But there NEED BE NO other taxes what bloody every.

AND a great deal of the effect of Douglas' national dividends and compensated price, COULD be attained by this means/ ratio between regular currency and S/S wd/ solve a good deal of Doug's problem. Anyhow people can undersatdn "NO TAXES" and they damn well wont understand the Brain Trust's[2] hooey.

Also NO DESTRUCTION OF FOOD stuff[3] until every man in the world is well fed.

That is all the PARTY PLATFORM you need.

IF you dont understand it/ I will explain. because it wd/ be better for you to understand it BEFORE you try to sell it to New York (and New York has got to buy it, before there is any more republican administration.)

Onnerstan your NO MORE bloody Bureaucracy/ can only be managed by tackling it from the CONSUMPTION (distribution) end/ and cutting out all this brine trust production and destruction bunk.

cordially

1. Arthur Griffiths (1872–1922) was an Irish politician who would not advocate Social Credit (Wilhelm 54). Pound quotes Griffiths in canto 19—"'Can't move 'em with a cold thing, like economics'"—which J. J. Wilhelm remarks is "one of the saddest refrains of the Pisan Cantos" (235).

2. The Brain Trust gave advice to Roosevelt about the economics of the depression when he was campaigning. Many members of the group later joined his cabinet (Schlesinger, *Crisis* 398–99). Pound had a serious problem with Roosevelt's reliance on the Brain Trust, as did others. One member, Raymond Moley, remarked that they would feed information to the president but added, "So far as I know he makes no effort to check up on anything that I or anyone else has told him" (qtd. in Kennedy 113).

3. During the depression, Secretary of Agriculture Henry Wallace ordered that crops and livestock be destroyed because farmers were unable to provide them at prices that the public could afford (Kennedy 204–5). On 22 March 1934, Borah argued in a speech that "80% of the world's population of two billion persons are today living below the poverty line. . . . Does not this present the problem of distribution rather than overproduction? In our own country there are no less than forty million people living below the poverty line. Shall we destroy food and the stuff of which clothes are made until we have taken care of our forty million?" ("Radio" 1).

14. POUND TO BORAH

TL-1, [Rapallo]

27 April 1935
HON
W.Borah

My Dear Senator

News this a/m of unexpected deferance on part of Senator from Louisiana. Waaal, brother, it is ON A PLATE, if Huey[1] and Cooglin[2] want you for presedent, and IF you will plug from sane economics, National dividend I2.50 a month paid in stamp scrip you just are the next president. Only you got to kiss Mr Mess Mellon, Vanderlip,[3] Barney Baruch and dear Mr Roosevelt's banker firiends Good BYE...

Two stinking reactionary groups and one active group, you are IN.

I trust some bright an improving licherchoor has been or is bein' sent you from London.

One danger is that F.D. MIGHT arise from the grave and do something intelligent FIRST. but that seems increasingly unlikely (unless you get news in Washington quicker than it it is let loose in Italy ù I mean American news.

Middle aged folks like me are about ready to prefer Mr Long to the pre ent administration.

Wall St/ is declining, it is about time for an American government.

BUT you got to cut loose from the Hooverite RUMP. NONE of THAT republican hog wash can be carried along. ask EZ, if doubt. (Hell. you CANT like people like Hoover and, in yr own interior KNOW you dont like 'em.

1. Huey Pierce Long (1893–1935) was a radical senator from Louisiana whom Pound admired a great deal, but who would be assassinated that coming September (Wilhelm 79). In his career, he was a popular figure and regularly appeared on the radio. His broadcasts received hundreds of letters of support. His

Share Our Wealth Society, which centered around the idea that "every man" should be a "king," claimed five million members. Long's ideas were similar to those of the very popular but controversial Father Charles E. Coughlin, and Long remarked, "Father Coughlin has a damn good platform" (qtd. in Kennedy 239).

2. Father Charles E. Coughlin was a popular, yet anti-Semitic, radio personality from the Shrine of the Little Flower in Detroit (Wilhelm 134). He believed that there was no such thing as overproduction as long as people were hungry and unclothed (Schlesinger, *Coming* 250). Pound supported him in the 4 July 1935 issue of the *New English Weekly:* "Anyone who has bothered to read Mr. Roosevelt's own volumes before opening Father Coughlin's will now find that the priest writes (speaks) better than the President. He has a respect for strictly American (U.S.A.) history.... He has taught 12 million Americans a number of valuable things which they didn't three years ago know" ("American Notes" 225). Even after Coughlin's anti-Semitism became more pronounced Pound continued to back him, claiming in the 12 March 1936 issue of the *New English Weekly* that "the most subservient bank pimp will be now unable to convince anyone that Coughlin is a mere rhetorician" ("American Notes" 425).

3. Frank Arthur Vanderlip (1864–1937) was the head of National City Bank and was a supporter of Irving Fisher's interests in stabilizing purchasing power. In 1933 he helped form the Committee for the Nation to Rebuild Prices and Purchasing Power, which was consulted by Fisher and George Warren (Schlesinger, *Coming* 198).

15. POUND TO BORAH

TL-3, [Rapallo]

23 [May] 1935
The Hon.
Wm Borah

My Dear Senator

Someday I may get you to realize that I got to Idaho before you did, and my septuagenarian father who is here with me, knew the state even earlier. You were born in quieter country.

I to d you months ago, when that dirty rag the Paris N/Y/ Herald accused you of boosting Hoover that the fat baby would NOT be a win in 1936. Now even the Phi(yes) ladelphia BANKERS have kicked the sloch in the jaw.

I am a very mild manner and orderly person, I haven't owned even an air gun since I was 14. but when I get so that I really want to shoot a g:d: human buzzard that fellow is getting to the point of NOT beling a political ass et.

I observe these internal boilings, just like a man in a laboratory does a test tube. When that tube bubbles, it don't mean the chemist has gone bug house.

How CAN pop Ickes[1] hand out that 5 billion save by per capita dividend?

Belgium (mi GORR BEL/gium has got to seeing that relief dont mean inventing jobs/ but increase in purchasing power of the whole people.

If Huey ever saw the enormous power of the possible stream of NEW MONEY (milk as opposed to killing and dividing the cow!!!

Oh, hell/ My granpop damn near put in Cleveland. I've still got his Letter on Blaine, that COUNTED in that election. I was in gallery <at tender age> (on the old man's ticket) when Matt Quay[2] adjourned the <Phila> convention, so they come in next day all lined up UNANimous McKinley and Teddy. and wuz the air full of happiness.

Don't think I have spent all my life deciphering mediaeval manuscripts.

The people are damn well FED UP with slimy and ambiguous crooks/ also with Morgenthaus, Baruchs, Mordecai Ezekiels,[3] Lehman's[4] etc.

THREE serious thinks have been THUNK. One here in Italy which can't be transplanted/ C.H.Douglas' and Gesell's. neither of which is a FIXED anchored KORAN to be kissed and petrified.

BUT certain economic facts and possibilities are KNOWN, and damn'd if the people are going to be hoaxed ON THOSE POINTS much longer.

An HONEST third party; or a republican party that means to GO HONEST (meaning CUT off its bum)

am moved by caricature of 3bnd/ party in Reid's rag/[5] which I do not buy, and wont as long as they print Lippmann,[6] but which I occasionally see.

Roosevelt is on the skids because he wont buck the banks. It dont matter a damn wht anybody thinks is POLITICS the people want decent economics.

If you want to go straight, I'm with you, and I will work on collecting facts/

AND if anything I say is an error I want to know it, and correct it.

Blokes like Warburg,[7] just lay down and CAN'T answer.

Dont let the stabilization guys fool you. They know quite a lot/ but Gesell knew more.

Purchasing power must be ADEQUATE... that is the FIRST requestte/ after that ole doc Fisher[8] and doc Whoosis can figger out their decimals and millessimals. Gesell's criteria for monetary system are REAL. (Fisher and Cohrsson have quoted 'em in Stabilized Money,[9] also with a lot of d/n hooey ... nice, useful anthology ...)

I can't tell what Cutting's death means, Surely the appointment of Chavez[10] is an outrage?

though I suppose people want something for their MONEY ... even if it don't come from the pays d'origine.

See that you travel on the earth for a bit.

yrs

Time and Tide slipped in printing my note to Angell/[11] the bonnie Britons LIKE it.

    1. Harold Ickes was the secretary of the interior under Roosevelt and was head of the Public Works Administration. Costing about $5 billion the first year, this program would give every able worker a job (Schlesinger, *Coming* 294–95). The PWA was intended to reform and regulate industry because it supplemented other programs in a grand effort to spread work, stabilize wages, and reduce hours. To Pound, Ickes was the only redeeming force in Roosevelt's administration. In the 13 June 1935 issue of the *New English Weekly*, Pound noted, "If there is one man above all others who should be seeing [national dividend] as the one way of increasing the purchasing power of the whole people without rascality, that man is Sec. Ickes, America's last hope in the present administration" ("American Notes" 165).

    2. Matthew Quay (1833–1904) was a lawyer, state treasurer, and senator from Pennsylvania, where he had a great deal of political clout. He was known for his tariff work and for his political maneuvering skills ("Quay").

    3. As part of the U.S. Department of Agriculture since Harding's administration and serving as Henry Wallace's economic advisor, Mordecai Ezekiel helped draft the Agricultural Adjustment Act that promoted allotment (Schlesinger, *Coming* 37–51). Ezekiel was sometimes ridiculed by one of Pound's favorites, Father Coughlin (Leuchtenburg 120).

    4. Herbert Lehman was governor of New York in the 1930s. As part of his attack on the New Deal, Borah sent a telegram to Lehman congratulating him on resisting a proposal for more federal control over munitions finances (McKenna 307–8).

    5. Ogden Mills Reid (1882–1947) was the editor of the *New York Tribune*, which he combined with the *New York Herald* to make the *Herald Tribune*. In a letter to E. E. Cummings two months prior, Pound makes reference to him (Ahearn 61–62).

    6. Walter Lippmann, a *Herald Tribune* columnist, wrote a variety of books, such as *Drift and Mastery: An Attempt to Diagnose the Current Unrest* (1914), *The New Imperative* (1935), and *An Inquiry into the Principles of the Good Society* (1937). Pound regularly criticized Lippmann and was sometimes anti-Semitic in his attacks (Redman 243).

    7. James P. Warburg was a New York banker interested in monetary experimentation (Schlesinger, *Coming* 196). Pound recommended Warburg's book *Money Muddle* to Mussolini in 1934 to illustrate that conservative financiers were confused about the Great Depression (Wilhelm 77).

    8. An economist at Yale University, Irving Fisher (1867–1947) wrote such books as *Stamp Scrip* (with Hans R. L. Cohrsson) and *The Money Illusion* (with Herbert W. Fisher).

9. Pound is most likely referring to *Stable Money: A History of the Movement* (1934) by Fisher and Cohrsson. Fisher was concerned with stabilizing money and also wrote about the topic in *Stabilizing the Dollar* (1920). He argues that by stabilizing the dollar, purchasing power is stabilized. To stabilize money, he argues, the government must be able to increase or decrease the price of gold just as businesses can increase or decrease their prices. Therefore, any inflation will be counteracted by a rise or fall in gold worth, so that currency, not the price of gold, will be stable.

10. Dennis Chavez (1888–1962) won election to the New Mexico House of Representatives in 1922 and to the U.S. House of Representatives in 1930. An ardent New Dealer, Chavez made a bid for the U.S. Senate in 1934 but lost to Senator Bronson Cutting. There were allegations that the election was fraudulent, and on his way back from a trip to New York to address these allegations, Cutting's plane crashed and he died. Governor Clyde Tingley appointed Chavez to replace the senator ("Chavez").

11. Sir Norman Angell was an economist, an author, and a Nobel Peace Prize winner. Angell received a letter from Pound and sent it to *Time and Tide,* where it was published based on its "considerable interest, literary and psychological" (qtd. in Norman 328).

16. POUND TO BORAH

TL-1, [Rapallo]

30 August [1935]
Hon. W. Borah

My Dear Senator

The Petit Parisien yesterday had an interesting artcj/ giving you the Republican nomination for next year.

My congratilations (if true) I think I shall send the article to the White House, to stimulate thought.

I hope you have NOTICED the Alberta elections.[1] I suppose the late Sen. Cutting succeded in telling you something about Social Credit and C.H.Douglas, whom, as matter of fact, I think you met at a distrac distracted buffet supper, where the Maj. said very little.[2]

I have written one (and hope to publich TWO) articles on the sane and praiseworthy ideas burried in some of Bro. Long's speeches.[3] BUT what I ant to know is WHETHER you propose to come out for Social Credit before F.D.R's does, or afterward.

If you postpone it, it will be too late.

The crux might almost seem to be whether you CAN go social credit and get nominated. If you wait till after nomination, F.D. may have stolen it.

At any rate, you better mug up the subject, and find out what its all about.

cordially but judicially yrs.

1. In 1935 Alberta's Social Credit party won fifty-seven seats out of the sixty-three in the Legislative Assembly (Flory 79).

2. See letter 10.

3. In one of these articles, published in the 12 September 1935 issue of the *New English Weekly,* Pound argues that Long, a serious presidential threat to Roosevelt, wants a national dividend and quotes Long as saying, "Every family

to be furnished by the government a homestead allowance, free of debt, of not less than one-third the average family wealth of the country, which means at the lowest that every family shall have the reasonable COMFORTS of life up to the value of from $5,000 to $6,000" ("American Notes" 345). Pound also explains, "If Huey is not yet for the rigid secretariat version of Douglas, he is most certainly NOT OPPOSED to any social credit aim. And he is the NEXT American toward whom U.S. social credit educational effort should be directed" (345).

17. POUND TO BORAH

TLS-1, Rome

1 October 1935
Hotel Italia
ROME
The Hon
Wm Borah

My Dear Senator

Congratulations on as much as has been quoted of yr remarks on the league of Nations.[1]

The question of Abyssinia[2] is NOT whether the league wants etc/ or don't want

It is a question of whether ANY nation that doesn't crawl on its belly and take orders from London (from the most treacherous nation of earth) is to have the league used against it; is to suffer unlimited and unscrupulous blackmail, wangled by England.[3]

Re/ France, a recent issue of VU (no. 380; no date on clippings sent me) contains an article on Bank of France by Francis Delaisi, which ought to be in the hands of every senator and congressman who can read french.[4]

Practically the first clear exposition of why french politics are what they are, and why they have five ministries in a week etc.

Tri/part treaties Eng/ Fr/ Ital re/ Abys/ did NOT invite Abys/ to sign.

y:v:t:

Ezra Pound

1. Borah spoke about the League of Nations in a 22 September 1935 speech. He urged the United States to return to the "long-established" policy of "Peace, Commerce, and honest friendship with all nations—Entangling alliances with none" ("Senator" 4).

2. Just two days after Pound wrote this letter, on 3 October 1935, Mussoli-

ni would invade Abyssinia (now Ethiopia). Because both Italy and Abyssinia were members of the League of Nations, other members, many of them sure the aggression would lead to another war, debated what should be done. The Abyssinian emperor, Haile Selassie, requested help from the league (Harris 6). Sir Samuel Hoare of Great Britain assured the world that his country would use force if needed to control the situation. The League eventually agreed to impose sanctions on Italy, but Italy conquered the African country in May 1936 and withdrew from the League of Nations soon afterward. Many historians have argued that this invasion was a real "turning point," to borrow David Kennedy's phrase, in foreign relations. The Rome-Berlin Axis agreement was announced on 1 November 1936, and later that month Japan and Germany signed the Anti-Comintern Pact. Winston Churchill believed that the world's inability to stop Mussolini "played a part in leading to an infinitely more terrible war." Churchill thought that Germany and Japan were spectators who got a view of "Great Britain's degeneracy" (qtd. in Kennedy 397).

3. Leading up to and during the invasion, the United States struggled with a formal position on Italy's actions. Roosevelt and Cordell Hull wanted to remain true to the Neutrality Act but also wanted to prevent war. Because the United States was not a league member, Roosevelt and Hull could remain completely independent in their decisions. Many Italian papers, however, suggested that American support of sanctions was a result of pressure from British propaganda (Harris 96).

4. The editors of the *New English Weekly* called Francis Delaisi's article in *VU* a "remarkable publication." Delaisi revealed that all but one of the twelve directors of the Bank of France "command a bank or financial house." The *New English Weekly* considered the French publication *VU* a mix between *Sphere* and *Illustrated London News* (Verdad 288). Delaisi (1873–1947) shared some of Pound's concerns, such as preventing World War II (Burns 58). On 1 December 1935 Pound claims in the *New Democracy* that "Francis Delaisi is the first man who has written any modern French history" (121).

18. POUND TO BORAH

ALS-3, Aquila

10 October 1935
Hotl Italia Aquila.
as from Rapallo

My Dear Senator.

Not only is there an italian vote. but you can have perfectly clear conscience that 7 million of subjected population in Abyssinia will be benefitted by conquest.

No one who ignores the enormous advance in living conditions of the people in backward parts of Italy during the past five years has any right to judge Italy's acts & needs. —You were dead right re/ the league hypocrites. —one law for England & another for everyone else.[1] England is the ONLY nation that can drag war from Africa into Europe.

& the real force driving that way is evil as the root of hell. The rest petty. local, swinish.

Mere hampering of Italy useless. & full of danger for everyone.

Financial news practically admits Mussolini had to ACT now. He has stopped war in Europe repeatedly: & I believe got it into Africa as alternative. & the gun buzzards & bankers are trying to force it back into Europe.

yrs Ezra Pound

You cd. cert. make a declaration of <u>benevolent</u> neutrality stronger than F.D.R & in form to diminish league devilment.[2]

no <u>use</u> merely irritating Italy. & cotton cd. be used.[3] etc. etc. I dont need to teach you to suck eggs.

1. Pound is referring to a speech Borah gave on 22 September 1935. In it, he expressed to the public that the United States should not get involved in the war that was about to break in Europe. He insisted European nations were going to

enter into another war even though the depression in the United States was "brought on in a large measure by the World War." He claimed that although Americans were poor and hungry, Europeans nations were spending "great sums" on and making "vast profits" from war ("Senator" 3).

2. Roosevelt had decided to impose a "moral embargo," which meant that American businesses would get no help from the U.S. government if they traded with belligerents and the trade became problematic. Trying to adhere to the Neutrality Act, the United States considered this approach a subtle way to address the Italian-Abyssinian crisis without getting too involved. Business owners, however, found this policy vague, especially since the government did not mandate, but merely suggested, what should not be exported (Harris 79).

3. When U.S. politicians were deciding what "essential war materials" businesses should refrain from exporting, Cordell Hull excluded cotton from this list. Some thought that southern representatives had pressured Hull to keep their interests in mind. He received some negative publicity for his decision, but he insisted that the United States did not export enough cotton to warrant limiting its trade (Harris 89).

19. POUND TO BORAH

ALS-2, Aquila

[post 10 October 1935]
Hotl Italia Aquila.

My Dear Seanator.

If both you & F.D. stand for bankers bunk. a 3<u>d</u> party might both arise & win.

Recognition of a few facts known to Mr. T. Jefferson. & to all honest economists (in fact to economists above the status of employee or hired crap writer might just land you in the Executive mansion...

yrs
Ez Pound

to Wm Borah

A nation should not rent its own credit from lice.

20. BORAH TO POUND

TLS-1, Boise

30 October 1935
Ezra Pound
c/o Hotel Italia,
Rome, Italy.

Dear Pound:

Thank you for your several letters. I find when I am home I have less time to answer letters than when I am in Washington.

We have had a perfectly marvelous autumn, somewhat interrupted last night by a whiff of winter.

I agree fully with your view as to "Orders from London". That is the whole proposition.

I am always glad to get your letters.

                        Very sincerely,
                        William E. Borah

21. POUND TO BORAH

TL-2, Rome

[post 15 November] 1935
Hon. Wm Borah

My dear Senator

What is NOW wrong with the picture is the definition of Italy's activity in Abyssinia as war. I thought it was, and was sorry Italy had started, but the evidence which that cub Eden[1] KEPT out of court, or out of consideration at Geneva, plus what I have had viva voce from Rocke,[2] PLUS the way Italy has gone ahead, road building etc. educate one.

It was O.K. of Frankie to declare neutrality a few days before Gneva Geneva decided Italy was warful.BUT it was clever of the Brits. to jockey him into doing it.

By the time this reaches you the NEW BRITISH campaign of l lies and press influencing may be apparent. If NOT, WATCH it.

Nic Butler (absolutely the most poisonous american after Herbert Hoover) has been, as natrual, palling with Rist,[3] Banque of France, Gregory,[4] pimp of Bank of Eng.

For god's sake open it UP. Get Nye[5] into action again on guns AND the finance behind them.

Hull ought to get his salary from Mont Norman[6] and Morgan.[7] and NOT fed at public expense. Butler you are bound to have against you, openly or otherwise.

I wish to God a REAL issue, namely the nature of money, and the modus of issue, cd. get into I936 election.

dont see how the devil you can get the BAD republicans to work with the good one/ thence the strength of F.D.R.

Morgenthau a comic? or just a little sunday school boy (or Saturday) that lunches with the Banque.

GET IT that Tannery[8] has confessed to crime basicly the same as that for which Louis XVI was guillotined.

I enclose Rocke's letter. and one from my aged father regarding it. Rocke has seen plenty more not in the print.

Two secs. of Brit. embassy went off with copy of current <New> English Weekly (Nov. 14) to show Drummond.[9] whether they will have the nerve to do so after reading it I dunno. I told 'em it wd. be a daln good thing for him.

Wife of Bulgarian sec. says Drummond gets dewey eyed about children who have cruel nurses. (how SCOTCH!!)

U.S. ought to keep out of war, but damn sanctions FOR the sake of British and Parisian finance,[10] and SOME consideration of the state of Abyssinia AS IS, in distinction to British theory of how to be holy and grab the earth ought to percolate into U.S. govt. action.

1. Anthony Eden (1897–1977) was the foreign secretary of Great Britain and was a major figure in discussions about sanctions against Italy ("Eden"; Baer 20–23).

2. Carroll Terrell tells us that Rocke was an English colonel who was involved in the Italian-Abyssinian crisis (676). Tryphonopoulos and Surette write that Cyril Edmund Spencer Rocke (1876–1968) authored a profascist account of the Italian-Abyssian conflict entitled *The Truth about Abyssinia* (285).

3. Charles Rist was the deputy governor of the Bank of France (Sayers 198).

4. Sir Theodore Emanuel Gregory was a professor, author, and member of the Macmillan Committee on the gold standard.

5. In 1934, Senator Gerald Nye led an investigation to examine if bankers, including J. P. Morgan, and munitions companies played a role in bringing the United States into war (McKenna 348–49).

6. Sir Montagu Norman (1871–1950) was the governor of the Bank of England from 1920 to 1944. He advised a return to the gold standard in 1925, and he was seriously engaged in war and postwar finance ("Norman").

7. J. P. Morgan Jr. (1867–1943) was a banker and chairman of J. P. Morgan and Company. During the Pecora Committee investigation, he said he could not remember if he had paid income tax in 1930 (Schlesinger, *Coming* 435). Pound thought that his company was a "monopolistic tyranny" (Wilhelm 101). In canto 40 Pound writes, "Profit on arms sold to the government: Morgan / (Case 97) sold to the government the government's arms."

8. Jean Tannery (1878–1939) was the governor of the Bank of France. During France's franc crisis, Henry Morgenthau Jr. allowed the U.S. Treasury to

buy French gold at the usual rate. The market was supplied with dollars, and therefore the value of the franc was protected (Burns 54). Louis XIV was tried for treason, so Pound must consider Tannery's acts treasonous.

9. James Eric Drummond (1876–1951), the sixteenth Earl of Perth, was the first secretary-general of the League of Nations (1919–33). He made Geneva the political center for negotiations concerning European affairs, was ambassador to Italy (1933–39), and became a representative peer of Scotland in 1941 ("Drummond").

10. Britain and France were most involved in the league's deliberations about Italy since their colonial territories adjoined Abyssinia. However, the two countries were torn between controlling Italy's aggression and keeping the country as an ally against Hitler (Harris 7).

22. POUND TO BORAH

TL-2, [Rapallo]

[November 1935]

My Dear Senator

Judging from this morning's figures re gun sales to Abyssinia, I dare say you will be accepting my estimate that ENGLAND will stop selling munitions to belli-gerents when she see an unliklihood of PAYMENT. They want the Negus'[1] last gold etc. that will be their limit.

The habits of Abyssinians to victim tribes were SHOW Geneva but Geneva looked away.

Maj. Darley[2] also told England long ago, and as long as England thought of getting the place, salvery was abhorrent.

You might note that DECENT Englishmen have been against sanctions. The clean men of very different opinion. I have heard from several direct. Amery,[3] Chiozza Money.[4] Lansbury,[5] Grigg.[6]

Now Chamberlain[7] himself admits Abyssinia isn't civilized.

But the fakers; the profession peace bibbers, Gib. Murray[8] N.Angell, all the blighters who are IMPervious to fact are all out to kill Italy.[9]

Note the RESULTS of England's policy. A? the handing over of the people to League (i;e; to a bureaucracy hired by the bankers, french, english dutch bureaucracy with other nations pretty well excluded.

The absence of MANDATE, show by Riddel.[10] Clique of British snobs, wheedling blindly and suggesting that people do the "right thing". snob fight, in part.

Diplomats have had careers because they aren't TOO curious.

The result of SANCTIONS:

1. restriction of consumption (amid <world> abundance)

2. raise in price of petrol

3. Increase in Mitsui gun sales.

PUT some TEETH in Nye commission[11] and show what western Europeans hold MITSUI. I don't mean just a share here and there, but big HOLDINGS.

America shd/ KEEP OUT and NOT help the squeezers and starvers. London usury, Paris usury. the ROOT is financial.

cordially t yrs.

1. *Negus* means "king" in Abyssinian (Darkwah 20). Emperor Haile Selassie was known as "Negus Negesti" (the king of kings; Farago 61).
2. Major Henry Darley served in South Africa and World War I ("Darley").
3. Leopold Charles Maurice Stennett Amery (1873–1955) was a British statesman and journalist ("Amery").
4. Sir Leo George Chiozza Money (1870–1944) wrote *Riches and Poverty* about the economics of Britain.
5. One month prior (on 8 October 1935) George Lansbury resigned as leader of the British Labour party. He had been attacked for his pacifist views during the fierce debate about the League of Nations imposing sanctions on Italy (Hardie 45).
6. Sir Edward William Macleay Grigg (1879–1955) was the governor of Kenya from 1925 to 1930, and prior to that was the head of the colonial department at the *London Times*. In the *New Democracy* issue of 1 December 1935, Pound writes, "Men who have never agreed on any other mortal thing under heaven, have damned the Geneva wangles and wrigglings. Leo Chiozza Money has thrown columns of FACTS at the bankers. Grigg, ex-governor of Kenya, has told 'em facts about Africa; Lansbury declined to fall into the Tory trap" (122–23).
7. British Prime Minister Neville Chamberlain (1869–1940) was wrongly accused of being pro-Italian. He was in favor of sanctions but was more interested in bringing Italy back into the league and avoiding war ("Chamberlain").
8. Members of the League of Nations Union, a British pacifist voluntary society, believed that the war could be prevented via the League of Nations. Professor Gilbert Murray of Oxford served as chairman of the union's executive committee from 1923 to 1938 (Hardie 49–50).
9. On 18 November 1935, the league took serious action against Italy by imposing a second round of more severe sanctions (Harris 87–88).
10. In November 1935, as part of a committee (which included Britain's Anthony Eden) organized to put a direct export embargo on Italy, the Canadian representative Walter Riddell argued that more resources (oil, coal, iron, and steel) should be added to the embargo "in principle" (Baer 66–67).
11. Borah and Senator Gerald Nye were opposed to U.S. involvement in Italian and Abyssinian affairs. Then involved in his investigation of bankers and munitions companies, Nye realized that sanctioning Italy would not end the war (Baer 201–2).

23. POUND TO BORAH

TL-3, [Rapallo]

[December] 1935
Hon W.Borah

My Dear Senator

I am heartimy glad that you are standing for nomination, though I mistrust the antiquated remnants of dud socialism that probably cling to some "delegations" etc. Believing that the U.S. wd/ have been happier had Harding, Coolidge and especially fat Herbie, been shot at birth, I am (entirely apart from these candid emotional urges) convinced that any of the other proposed nominees wd/ be a cardboard set up. F.D. could certainly knock 'em dead, and that without much effort. (At least that it what it looks like on a damp Mediterranean evening.

Whether you can get the nomination on a platform containing ANY decent items, you know far better than I can.

And UNTIL the party has a platform with at least SOME decent feature I do not (candidly, in fact possibly MORE candidly than etiquette requires) know whether I prefer you to F.D.R.

After all he meant well, and I am damned if Hoover or Cooledge EVER had a decent intention or was or is capable of ANY decent volition toward the good of the WHOLE people.

As a means of weedin' out some of of the most pizinous barmints, I offer you the enclosed little implement. I combined it a couple of years ago and it WORKS. It may look as simple as Tugwell[1] BUT, after considerable trial I find that there are two results of the answers. I mean a man can't answer it without either

    1. a confession of ignorance

    2. telling the truth

OR 3. making an ass of himself, of such an obvious nature that a number of people can be SHOWN that that IS what he is.

I am NOT suggesting that YOU answer 'em. In fact I hope you WON'T until you are definitely nominated. But I shd/ be very glad to have the questions shoved about where Hoover, Landon[2] other hetroclite nuissances AND the reigning house, would be impelled or cornered into trying to answer them. (no need of my name staying on 'em.)

I don't hold ANY theories about money that I am not ready to drop if anyone can and will stand up and SHOW that I am in error.

The correspondence between the economists whom I think are clear headed is developing.

I had twelve pages from Mc Nair Wilson[3] in reply to my critique to my letter on his "Defeat of Debt"

And that is only one item.

Good things in that book. Especially the figures on P.78. Of strangle of Germany and Italy, when forced to get Sterling Exchange. (Wilson says Hoare[4] referred to these in Sept.) and then pore Sammy fell.

Eden is the son in law of the Westminster Bank so THAT mystery is largely explained. It has taken me a shameful time to find this out. father in law Sir Gervase Beckett[5] havent had time to trace what that means in detail.

In I923 the young swine both married and became an M/P/ nacherly hiz rize wuz rapid.

Manchester Guardian, Whitwood, not Whitworth chemicals.[6] Evening Standard, Birmingham Small Arms.[7]

the colour of the British press shd/ ALWAYS be charted.

Hope they sent you New Democracy for Dec. I.[8]

No sign that Townsend[9] means ANYthing, at least nothing yet recd. here.

What the DEUCE is <Senator> Bankhead? How the devil can any man get hold of an idea and keep it three years without getting down deeper INTO it??? or doing anything to develop it, or see what is missing in the first draft of it??

At any rate, best wishes for Happy New Year (PLUS) I hope you will run, so that electorate will at least have some sort of real ISSUE to vote on.

very sincerely yours

1. Professor Rexford G. Tugwell of Columbia was an authority on agriculture and was a member of Roosevelt's Brain Trust (Schlesinger, *Crisis* 110, 399).

2. Governor of Kansas Alfred Landon would defeat Borah and become the Republican presidential nominee in 1936.

3. Robert McNair Wilson (1882–1963) was a surgeon and a writer with whom Pound corresponded between 1934 and 1958. Pound was particularly impressed with his book on finance, *Promise to Pay: An Inquiry into the Principles and Practice of the Latter-Day Magic Called Sometimes High Finance* (Walkiewicz and Witemeyer 142). On page 78 of in *Defeat of Debt*, Wilson discusses the stiff competition American wheat farmers had to face when going into English markets after France, Italy, and Germany "dumped enormous quantities of wheat" into Britain. He also refers to a speech that Sir Samuel Hoare gave to the League of Nations in September 1935 which addressed the pressure Germany, France, and Italy were under to obtain sterling credits.

4. Sir Samuel Hoare (1880–1959) would resign as the British foreign secretary of state in 1935 because he was criticized for the abortive Hoare-Laval pact of 8 December 1935. The pact would have allowed Mussolini to keep certain territories and would have given Abyssinia sovereign rights over an outlet to the sea (Hardie 169–71).

5. Sir Gervase Beckett (1866–1937) was the director of Westminster Bank and Anthony Eden's father-in-law (Burns 62).

6. Philip J. Burns suggests that Whitworth Chemicals was a Vickers-Armstrong subsidiary that had taken over Armstrong-Whitworth, another armaments company (62). Pound's reference to Whitwood is obscure, but perhaps he is referring to another munitions company or to a bank named Whitwood. He may also mean Whitwood, England.

7. Birmingham Small Arms was a British munitions company (Burns 62).

8. In the 1 December 1935 issue of *New Democracy* Pound argues a number of points that he would have wanted Borah to consider. Pound writes that Mussolini had prevented war a number of times and observes that since Britain was involved in a slave trade for centuries it was in no position to judge Italy's treatment of the Abyssinians.

9. In 1934 Dr. Francis Townsend founded the Old Age Revolving Pensions, Ltd., which later took shape as a bill in Congress. Under this plan people over sixty years of age would receive a monthly pension funded by a 2 percent national tax. It did not directly lead to the Social Security pension, but it brought the same issues into the spotlight. Pound was not in favor of Townsend's plan (Walkiewicz and Witemeyer 92).

24. POUND TO BORAH

TLS-5, Rapallo

1935
Hon/ Wm Borah

My Dear Senator

If you can stand "for the constitution" on the HONEST issue, that Congress has power over issue of currency, I.E. if you can line up industray against usury, you've got a show for 1936.

PLUS Hull who is enough to sink any administration. If F/D/R straddels from sycophancy to England to flatter of communist prejudice against "fascist Italy" that puts him in dilemma like yours (which at least from here, seems to be the straddle from honest republicans mostly in the West, to the old Wall St. crottin.

all of which you know, but mayn't be loss of postage stamp to get confirmation, from perspective.

You are sound on the swindle of Geneva. I never can make out whether ANY American in the U.S. EVER sees ANY European papers. Certainly the real papers that run against the hired lies, do NOT reach centres of power of power

Does the French Ambassador in Washington KNOW that England quite probably CAN NOT put an army into the field?

Can England, anyhow?

France is run by the 12 regents of the Banque (hereditary in fact, tho not in theory), three govt. straw men cover this and could be shot by popular justice without DeWendel and the other eleven getting caught. Hence British blackmail via the Banque / and Laval's[1] discomfort.

England could and shd/ clean up her INTERNAL filth. The U.S.A ought NOT to help the dirtiest set of swine in London.

all this ought to be good politics, and NON COMMITTAL so far as Republican platform is concerned.

Naturally I wish to heave I had some idea of WHAT you wd. do if you got IN, and how far you cd. go toward getting IN IF you had any intention of doing anything useful.

Nomination might be hardest job, and the double crossing if you promised ANY honest monetary investigation between nomination and Nov. next.

Can't you offer Hull a baronetcy <(>or something real English. (Parenthesis have just taken a breater to open the subject with him; It is NOT a polite or politic act and I suppose some rubber stamp will keep him from getting the letter.

Pity my knowledge of Europe can't be some use to the nation.

Anything you'd like me to say in ESQUIRE?[2] You can't buy it, and you can't bend it.

I cd. make money by doing several odd jobs.

(Writing crap for the utilities, NOO KAY/rear fer young men.)

Have YOU looked into the money system; or tried to find out WHY England supports slavery? now as in 1861 or the time of Hawkins?[3]

50 bullied nations/ fearing England, debtor nations or banklans about to borrow.

Capt. Goldoni from the front "We have had no battles, we have all joined in and made Roads.[4]

Even the slimy Hoare dont deny that Abyssinia wd/ be better under Italian rule.

HAVE you see the evidence of what slave trade MEANS? Has the bleating Brit/ public. often well meaning, but IGNORANT,adn kept igno ant.

You will never TEACH a better method, as long as the main purpose of Eng/ govt. is to hide the MONSTROUS fake and evil of the usury system

And the attempt to starve Italy, for the sake of crushing the Duce over a technical quibble is large scare crime than any implied in colonial settlement.

Justice has one set of weight not six, not one for Germany, one for Japan, and another for Italy.

also AFGAN frontier?

RESULTS of Brit/ blindness/ spread of sanctions FROM half the british population;

i;e; FURTHER restriction of consumption

[illegible line]

RESULTS of not strangling that pig Eden in his cradle/

1 Restriction of consumption

2. Rise in price of petrol.

3. sale of munitions by Mitsui/ in WHICH jap/ firm europeans are INTERESTED, and HOW!!

That is British policy.

Ezra Pound

1. Pierre Laval was the French foreign minister and deputy premier (Hardie 58).

2. Pound wrote for *Esquire* during this period (Heymann 69).

3. Sir John Hawkins (1532–95) was an English naval administrator and commander. He began his career as a merchant in the African trade and was an early slavetrader ("Hawkins"). Pound thought that Britain was being hypocritical in supporting an African country and reminds his readers in *New Democracy* that "In 1562 John Hawkins sold 300 negroes" ("Who" 122). Hawkins was well known for that 1562 voyage ("Hawkins").

4. Goldoni was probably an Italian officer. His remark would serve Pound's purpose in trying to argue that Italy was not conquering Abyssia but rather "civilizing" it.

25. POUND [TO BORAH]

TL-[1], [Rapallo]

[1935]

[line(s) missing]

another takinb Wallace[1] mushy soul out and dry cleaning it a third puffing the George Horrace Lorrimer[2] Tugwell up till his fat mugg busts.

similar technique cd. <//> be applied to Langdon and co. IF the country shits itself into electing 'em.

This means more coherence and harder WORK by the contributors than Money has yet demanded.

I also suggest that criticism of Social Justice be constructive from now on, rather than destrictive. That the points on which Coug and co/ are right/ and assume that the follies in the paper are due to slips; to hurry of weekly issue etc.

WE MUST have larger coalition. Do you see ANY sound elements in the Republican party or the EXTREME right in the House of Reps.???

I mean patriots who will stand FOR the WHOLE constitution; even when it runs counter to what they have accepted from HABIT. meaning ALSO the banks. I mean some good guys have tolerated Wall t. BEACUESE they didn't notice it was unconstitutional.

yrs.

1. Henry Agard Wallace was the secretary of agriculture and was also the vice president of a group of economists and businessmen assembled by Irving Fisher called the Stable Money Association (Schlesinger, *Coming* 198).

2. George Horace Lorimer (1868–1937) was an American journalist and editor-in-chief of the *Saturday Evening Post* from 1899 to 1936 (Edwards and Vasse 130).

26. POUND TO BORAH

TL-2, [Rapallo]

[1934–36]
The Hon
WM.Borah

My Dear Senator:

In case you might like to see what it looks like in Woptalian. All the press have spoken well of yr/ speech and the Mercantile[1] has given it front page.

There is ANOTHER aspect. Not only ought Americans to avoid getting slaughtered for the Becketts and Sasoons[2] BUT it ought forever to be impossible for Tannery or any other g:g: frog bank-pimp to go up to Basel[3] and tell the congester usury gang that he had got AID from the American Treasury (meaning Morgenthau unenlightened by Strauss[4]) and from the Tank of England
TO PREVENT A POLITICAL CRISIS.

That is NOT stating out of European entanglements, that is very DIRTILY aiding a straw man (acting for a gang of bloody crooks) to betray the french people.

I think Frank D/ has done some good work and both YOU and HE are up against very hard handicaps but that Sec/ of the Treausury[5] is no damn good.

And kikie Strauss is no good either. Business of an Ambassador to prevent incompetent ASS in cabinet from committing that kind of mess.

Heaven knows if you can clean enough of the MUCK out of the Rep/ party to get nominated/ and if so....???

waaaaal?!?!!!

However I recommend (entirely apart from my having dug it out) I recommend the summary of what T.Jefferson knew about bank muck, as concentrated in chap XXX of my Jeffrsn/ Mussolini.[6]

One party and/or BOTH ought to put those five pages into their platform.

and may the best man win.

cordially Yrs

1. *Il Corriere Mercantile* was an Italian magazine published in Genova.

2. Pound accused the Sassoon family of controlling the opium trade in the Far East (Casillo 230). Pound would later contend that British soldiers should not die for Victor Sassoon (Heymann 116).

3. Basel, Switzerland, is very close to both France and Germany and was the home of the Bank of International Settlements.

4. Jesse Straus (of Macy's department store), along with Henry Morgenthau Sr., gave money to the Roosevelt campaign (Schlesinger, *Crisis* 280). Pound probably disliked him for being Jewish, a businessman, and a supporter of Roosevelt.

5. Henry Morgenthau Jr. was the secretary of the treasury.

6. In chapter 30 of *Jefferson and/or Mussolini*, Pound writes that "national control of the national finances" existed during Washington's administration but that it "ceased when the administration changed WITHOUT there being a corresponding change in the control of the bank" (117).

27. POUND TO BORAH

TL-1, [Rapallo]

2 January [1936]
Hon. Senator Wm Borah

My Dear Senator

Very astute speech by Roosevelt at Atlanta Three years Social Credit hammering AND he now admits that The mass of American people eat third class diet because they HAVE NOT THE PURCHASING POWER to get more and better food.[1]

But he offers false dilemma/ the dirty old clothes of England/ DOLE,[2] based on pity (or fear the starved will git nasty) AND public works on fascist model.

It wd. be betrayal of the people to sabotage the campaign against child labour[3] (partly?? successful???) and SOME of the work's schemes.

BUT the dilemma is FALSE. The second question on my Volitionist list is NOT faced.[4]

The DIVIDEND is based on justice. It is NOT a hand out/ it is not a reward to laziness or incapacity (produced more or less by sloth). It is based on justice/ and its MAIN aim is to bring the TOTAL purchasing power of the people Up the AVAILABLE wanted goods. i;e; LIFE, life of trade, sane economy.

Go to it Brother.

Also F.D.R. has heard of USURY. Good, and high time. You beat him to PARTAGGIO.[5] (Esquire only costs 50 cents).

1. In that speech of 20 November 1935 in Atlanta Roosevelt said, "National surveys which have been conducted in the past year or two prove that the average citizenship of the United States lives today on what the doctors would call a third-class diet." He continued: "Why are we living on a third-class diet? Well, the best answer I know is this: The masses of the American people have not the purchasing power to eat more and better food" (Roosevelt 473).

2. In the early thirties a distribution of food, money, and clothing to the needy in Great Britain was called a "dole." This was referred to as "charity," especially if given by the government. Many opposed it, believing it had caused the British depression (Schlesinger, *Crisis* 178–80). In the *New English Weekly* from 26 October 1933, Pound writes that "if the British Dole, or a small fraction of it, had been paid in stamp-script, two thirds of England's worries would have been solved" ("Stamp Script" 32).

3. In the early thirties child labor was becoming a problem again (Schlesinger, *Coming* 90).

4. In "Volitionist Economics" from the 15 November 1934 issue of *New Democracy*, Pound declares that nations should not go into debt by creating wealth, several countries already have purchasing power, a nation should have two types of currencies (domestic and international), money should be certificates for work done, taxation should fall on currency itself, money should be issued against a commodity up to the amount of the commodity that the public wants, economists should change their terms to reflect reality more accurately, and monopolies should not interfere in the business of private citizens (105).

5. *Partaggio* was a medieval term that signified the sharing of profits in a collaborative enterprise. In "Gold and Work" Pound writes, "The distinction between production and corrosion has been lost; and so has the distinction between the sharing-out of the fruits of work done in collaboration (a true and just dividend, called *partaggio* in the Middle Ages) and the corrosive interest that represents no increase in useful and material productive of any sort" (351).

28. POUND TO BORAH

TLS-3, Rapallo

12 March 1936

Hon Senator Wm Borah

You can never come to accord with New York, Al Smiff and Hoover (who represent the same form of excrement) and you couldn't look yrself in the face if you did.

BUT you might do something with Boston. What I know about Tinkham[1] is what I have seen in the papers plus the fact he occasionally gives a straight answer. He DISlikes several things a male of the species OUGHT to dislike.

If you have anything ON him, spill it. BUT you build solider on a real man than on a damn crook.

I suppose he is regarded as reactionary?? But I do NOT think he is a crook. AND economics are so simple ONCE a man means to run STRAIGHT, that I believe you, Tinkham and Coughlin (as apparent in his speeches since Jan Ist.) cd. work out an agreement. I shd/ suggest that it be gone over by Larkin's[2] accountants. Crate L's stationary looks anything but excentric. If you've got a business of that size you don't play it out on sheer folly.

Hen. Ford. Hitler, Kozul, minister of building in Jugoslavia,[3] ALL agreed on certain solid TRUTH, so is Daladier[4] and Duboin[5] <deputé> (Ligue du Droit du Travail[6] having meetings in Salle Wagram,[7] <crowd of> 5000 every two weeks.)

Crate L/ said you were willing to see him but that he cdn't get to Washington <at that time> and had suggested that you see Nyland.[8] I don't know that that substitution is wholly satisfactory. Not that I have anything against Nyland, save that he may (mind I dont say he IS) be interested in managing things instead of interested in the IDEA. All of which MAY give him driving force, and wd/ make him useful campaign worker ... you'll need several different temperaments in that show.

Anybody ON the ground see a stronger Republican line up than Borah AND Tinkham??

I am not dogmatizing. I am tryin' to see the U.S. I936 in perspective, historic process etc// You can't run with a man who is merely a weaker edtn of Wm. B.

WHAT else do you see on the East coast that you cd/ trust with a tin of sardines??

I don't mean ole Geo/ wd. partikiler LIKE sittin' still in the Senate.. but still...

If you dont like the idea, get out yr/ congressional directory and go thru the dn/ thing with a pin, and a bandage over yr/ eyes.

Get an Easterner who wont sell you out to Strauss and Lamont fer the price of a pair of breeches.

reverently yrn/

EZ P.

vide P/S/

P/S/

IF you ever opened that "Jefferson and/or Mussolini" that I told my pubr/ to send you AND if you thought me a gorDamn fool WHEN you read it, I suggest that you notice the Italian Bank Reform (probably NOT widely advertised in the financial press) IN RELATION to page II7 of that estimable vol. by the undersigned. particularly the pp/ folowing the Phrase "While the government remained at Philadelphia."[9]

Even the 'Corriere della Sera'[10] has got round to saying "in view of date when it wuz written might seem to have an <u>alone profetico</u>/ meanin' "breath of prophercy abaht it." in our mama tongue

Yuh/ had orter read chap XXX ANYHOW. I can tell you or any bloke to do that, without personal vanity as that chapter is all Mr T.Jefferson. AN I hear itz struck spaaaks in texAS.

     v Ez Pound

 1. George Holden Tinkham was a congressman from Massachusetts and a favorite of Pound. Pound's "three most sustained correspondences" in the

American political realm were with Borah, Senator Cutting, and Representative Tinkham (Pearlman 419).

2. Pound's correspondent James Crate Larkin was a businessman, a director of the National Social Credit Association in New York, and the author of a book about Social Credit entitled *From Debt to Prosperity: An Introduction to the Proposals of Social Credit* (Walkiewicz and Witemeyer 153).

3. M. Kozul was the minister of building in Yugoslavia. In the 2 April 1936 issue of the *New English Weekly*, Pound claims that Kozul was "ON" and "fighting for stamp scrip" ("American Notes" 489).

4. Edouard Daladier was the premier of France and was a Radical party leader (Redman 185).

5. The economist Jacques Duboin argued that people lost jobs because of the mechanical age (Burns 73). Pound considered him a Social Crediter and in the 20 February 1936 issue of the *New English Weekly* translates extensive passages from Duboin's work, such as this: "For every augmentation of the means of production, there should be a corresponding augment of the means of consumption" ("Jacques" 92).

6. The League for the Right to Work was a French organization that Pound favored. He translates its main argument in the *New English Weekly* issue for 20 February 1936: "'The mere fact of a man's being alive gives him the right to live. Civilized man can not have LESS rights' (meaning 'natural rights') 'than a savage.'" Pound explains that the league demands that every man have his share of work, his share of leisure, and his share of produced riches ("Jacques" 92–93).

7. Salle Wagram is a convention center in France.

8. Along with Larkin, W. A. Nyland was a director of the National Social Credit Association in New York ("Fighting" 122).

9. In *Jefferson and/or Mussolini,* Pound writes about what the banking system was like in "Federal hands, i.e., as opposed to Jefferson" and remarks, "While the government remained at Philadelphia a selection of members of both Houses were constantly kept as directors who, on every occasion interesting to that institution, or the *views of the federal head* voted at the will of that head; and together with the stock-holding members, could always make the federal vote that of the majority" (117).

10. *Corriere della Sera* was a periodical originating in Milan (Walkiewicz and Witemeyer 74).

29. POUND TO BORAH

TL-1, [Rapallo]

22 February [1937]

My Dear Senator

Lard Beaverbrook's London DAILY EXPRESS on the 20th inst. referred to you as shylock No. I. <& 2.>

That's O.KAY. Couldn't be better. Bully for you and keep AT it.

The bastards are sore that Runciman didn't run away with more of Morgenthau's chestbuts.

NOTE that "the invisible man" Runcy had with him Neimeyer, and that this in itself wd/ constitute a good reason for breaking off ALL diplomatic relations with England.[1]

EVEN if Herb the swine did send Mellon as Ambassador to London, when the old skinflint ought to have been in jug.

F.D.R. did a fine bit of work when he refused to see Kike Norman and Norman had to see M/ in Maine, Got to hand him that/

But to refuse England's public enemy No. I. and then have his back door shyster and pet boy sent over officially is NO cause for amity with England.

The foetor of their present gang is unutterable.

Nevertheless I believe I have a word or two on it in the GLOBE new magazine[2] which they say was published in St Paul the day before yesterday.

1. British statesman Walter Runciman and the director of the Bank of England, Otto Ernst Niemeyer, visited the United States in late January 1937. There was wide speculation that their visits were planned to coincide so they could work out an agreement between Great Britain, France, and the United States on currency stabilization. In actuality, each had a separate agenda (Burns 110).

2. Between 1936 and 1959 Pound wrote a series of letters to the *Globe*, a small magazine out of the Minneapolis–St. Paul area ("Ezra"). I tried to obtain the specific article to which Pound refers but was unable to locate it.

30. POUND TO BORAH

TL-2, [Rapallo]

15 December 1937
Wm. Borah
U.S.Senate

My Dear Senator

I don't know whether you take any interest in electing a republican president in 1940. The subject is worth a little thought. In fact I have meditated on it for some time.

Staring with a hope that you wd. stand in 1936, but recognizing your wisdom in NOT trying to beat F.D.R. at that time.

Also New York would have double crossed you, and NEVER will do anything else.

The nomination of Landon, an utter noodle, may have convinced even the bankers that the people wont stand a complete drivveling idiot.

I dont believe the republicans can put in a Westerner. I know of only ONE Easterner who cd/ carry the West.

He has NOT been developed. He has a record that COULD swing the people. You may think that I am too far away to see anything. But I want you at least to let yr/ mind run over this matter: You senators may not have looked into the lower house.

That god damned fake the League of Nations is now BUST. You and Uncle George TINKHAM did a damn good job keeping us out of it. Lodge[1] and Knox[2] ae no longer with us. The country OUGHT to wake up to Tinkhams little known work at that time.

ALSO to Uncle George's battle against the prohibition idiots/

I am not a complete idiot: So far as I know no one has thought of G.H.T. as a possible nominee.

Americans so damn SELDOM think of anything. Look at Frankie's cabinet (mostly with the french significance of the term). Perkins,[3] paralyzed in the neck and thence upward. Morgenthau that cdn't run an apple farm, Wallace, god' owen belove BOOB, next to Landon, who of course is unbeatable, much as Wallace folly distresses me, he never touched Landon's low. Whatever narsty pieces of work are in the Republican wigwam, you haven't Barney Baruch as a liability.

I dont say th old elephant can get over the fence. But I do honestly believe Uncle George COULD stir whatever decency is left in the country.

Have a shot at thinking it ove, and/or write to me if you think I am an especially blated damn fool.

cordially yours

1. Henry Cabot Lodge (1850–1924) was chairman of the Senate Foreign Relations Committee and opposed the League of Nations (McKenna 152).

2. Philander C. Knox was the secretary of state under Taft and opposed the League of Nations (McKenna 157).

3. Frances Perkins was Roosevelt's secretary of labor (Schlesinger, *Coming* 2). In the 10 January 1935 issue of the *New English Weekly* Pound calls her a "peril to the nation" ("American Notes" 270).

31. POUND TO BORAH

TL-1, [Rapallo]

13 January 1939
BRAVO, BORAH

My Dear Senator

KEEP AT IT. What every decent man in Europe WANTS is a sane Europe and NO WAR west of the Vistula.[1]

It is damned hard to get this simple statement into print in America. Even small magazines DELAY what I send when they print it at all. Dislike war, but the practical move is to keep it OUT of Europe/

Indibitably the drive for war last year was from gunbuzzards/ Rothschild[2] implied/ I shd/ still like to know WHICH half of Skoda[3] was sold to Anglo-xyz a few days ago. If the frogs owned THAT half and Rothschild the OTHER half, the cui prodest of the Czek-Slovak attempts to blow up Europe is fairly clear.

Here's to the next president and may he not be a democrat.

As to ambassadord/ Bill Bullett[4] is capable of seeing with jew colouring, and I wdn't trust Kennedy[5] with a six pence.

cordially yours

1. The Vistula River flows mostly through Polish territory.
2. The House of Rothschild was a group of international banks owned by the Rothschild family that ruled the money markets in Europe for most of the nineteenth century (Edwards and Vasse 187). Many countries borrowed money from these banks to pay debts, fund projects, or wage wars ("Rothschild"). During the twentieth century, the House was not as influential, but the family still held a great deal of power and socialized with politicians and diplomats (Wilson 365).
3. Skoda started as a Czech steelworks and forging plant and soon became the largest armament manufacturer in the Austro-Hungarian Empire. Skoda continued to manufacture arms during both world wars ("History").

4. William C. Bullitt (1891–1967) was the U.S. ambassador to France.

5. Joseph P. Kennedy (1888–1969) was an influential backer of Roosevelt and was the U.S. ambassador to Britain. He and Bullitt were key players in the events leading up to World War II.

Appendix A: Related Letters

POUND TO THE *Hailey Times*

Hailey Times, *Hailey, Idaho, 18 June 1931, 38–39*

Poet Ezra Pound, born in Hailey, writes from his home in Rapallo, Italy, in his own characteristic style, to send greetings to the folks now living in the place of his birth, and to give wings to some caustic criticisms.

"From Far Away Italy Come Greetings to Hailey Folks"
by Ezra Pound

The Hailey Times:

Replying to yours of 4th inst: Am I to congratulate the town on being five years older than I am?

My memories of the region are not very clear. Tales I have heard, about the deacons collecting the parson's salary over the bars of the 24 saloons that bordered the street.

When I met Chas. E. Scott Wood[1] in Paris he said in his day Hailey wasn't a town, but that old man Hailey was driving a stage coach.

The only Haileyan I have even seen outside my own family was an ambassador who seemed to have found his last job rather wearing. He had energy enough to help me against one of those damnable lice that Woodie Wilson stuffed into every American passport office in Europe and from whom Senator Borah has done nothing to deliver us.

I strongly suggest that Borah be made to carry a little certificate saying who he is, and that every time he crosses a state line he has to have it stamped by an official of the state department or some other pestilent moron. Passports were revived by a Democratic administration. The great people howl when some grafter in Washington steals a few thousand bucks, but when some idiot causes the American traveling public to lose $5,000,000 a year by paying visa fees to foreign governments, for which the American traveling public gets nothing, the great peepul lap it up like warm moonshine.

The only thing I have against my native state is Senator Borah as head of a senate committee to deal with foreign countries about which he knows nothing and where he has never set foot.

As for a message to my native town—How can I tell what the citizens want to know? I suggest they study agricultural credits and that the town library tank up on books dealing with same. There is also a chapter on the "Working Day"[2] concealed in a long book by an unpopular author. That would be good stuff to give the young boys in the schools. It would make good insides for your paper.

I can never understand why local editors in America can't run just as good literary stuff as we run in our little Genova paper. Are the mountaineers less capable of mental effort than the swarthy Italians?

Rapallo, Italy,
May 23, 1931

1. Charles Erskine Scott Wood (1852–1944) was an American fiction writer who wrote such books as *The Poet in the Desert*.

2. "The Working Day" is a chapter in *Das Capital* by Karl Marx (1818–83). Although Marx was no favorite, Pound sometimes referred to his writings. In the *New English Weekly* issue of 13 June 1935, Pound writes about Marx's exploration of child labor in mills.

HOMER POUND TO BORAH

ALS-2, Rapallo

26 February [1936]
<E.P.>
<radio>

My Dear Senator.

My son Ezra has just called my attention to the Italian paper "La Stampa and its article on your speech. "Borah denuncia l'ipocisia inglese" and suggests I send you copy of the paper. I have done so; but I would like you to favor me with a copy of it in English if you will kindly do so.

We have been very much interested in hearing that you were likely to be the nominee on the "Republican Ticket" for President, and I would also be glad if you could send me any news confirming same. As Ezra was from Hailey, and I have always had and still have been interested in news from "The 'Gem' of the Mountains" it will be great if Idaho should have a President from there.

You may have read some of my son's articles or books. He had a letter a short time ago from Senator Pope,,[1] &. & Knowing that you are a very busy man, I will refrain from taking up more of your time.

                    Sincerely yours
                    Homer L. Pound.

"P.S. First Register US Land Office Hailey Idaho 1883=appointed by President Arthur."

   1. James Pope was a senator from Idaho who fully supported the New Deal (McKenna 343).

POUND TO TINKHAM

TL-4, [Rapallo]

11 March [1936]
The Hon. Geo. H.Tinkham
Washington D.C.

Dear Mr Tinkham

I am for "Tinkham 1940". And I am not writing this letter frivolously. I am not interested in impossibilities and I believe I have for months carried on a more searching correspondence with the best economists than anyone else has had the gumption to attempt.

I have been on the job for 18 years, and 12 years ago I came here (Italy) to see the difference between what blokes write in a high brow weekly and what gets DONE.

Most writers on econ/ are laboratory men. They make blue prints, and have NO imagination. I mean they do NOT visualize humanity, Bill, Joe, and Henry DOING the things on the program.

Most of 'em cant use WORDS. I mean they do not start by defining their terms, and continue by sticking to CLEAR definitions.

One of the most lucid of 'em, and a man who is READ by govt. advisors has just written me "credit is debt"

Oh yeah, and east is WEST, and left is right.

Sure, he MEANS something, but by the time he has utte<u>re</u>d it isn't there.

<ANOTHER CASE> Peeke,[1] I think the blokes name is, writes a buttery article about F.D.R. contribution to the "pure science of mathematics" and suddenly shifts from talking about NUMBERS (arithmetic) to dollars.

Hollis[2] writes of prices being STABLE for two centuries when prices were steadily declining AS MEASURED in metal. which was what they thought they were measuring by.

The job of building up a clean terminology GOES ON. We've got plenty of high brow magazines and Butchart's "MONEY3"[3] is a start for a new library. Butch. being the second generation brought up, as you may say, by Orage,[4] E.P. and Douglas.

Daladier, Duboin (of Ligue du Droit du Travail) Rossoni,[5] Kozul in Jugoslavia, Hen. Ford recently, and EVEN Hitler in one clause of his last outbreak all see certain F FACTS.

If it were a mere matter of laboratory work, I wdn't be impelled to buy the postage stamp on this letter.

I am now after what you and Bill Borah can DO. If, that is, you are interested, and want a program that will WORK.

I don't know what you think of Borah. Hoover is a crook and the other possible candidates for I936 are DEAD and petrified from the neck up.

The problem in dynamics is Tinkham I940. IF G.H.T. will consider sane monetary reform WITHIN the frame of the Constitution. and without LOWERING anyone's standard of living. (though that phase of it question is probably above and outside popular politics.)

You'd probably have to nominate Borah. YOU, and not the expansive Wm B. wd. have to make terms. That is to say YOU wd/ have to put the DEFINITE ideas into him. or make him sign 'em.

There is no use in expecting any great precisions from him. (At least damn'd if I see it.)

on my part it means working on private letters to you rather than in splashing ideas over printed pages.

I don't mean I wd. quit publishing economic articles, but there wd/ have to be coordination, and the mere pleasure of uttering ideas, wd. have to be fitted into the probable effect of printing them.

Lenin saw Mussolini as the one man who cd/ get anything DONE in Italy.

It is the Boss's genius for seeing what must be day by day. What done FIRST. March I936/ what done next after that April; May, June.

That is the kind of thought (or imagination to use a word which Napoleon occasionally found useful) which is needed.

Borah election or non-election etc. needn't mean postponing a sane economic reform. There is no reason why you shouldn't come in I940, emeritus, on the gratitude FOR having got it done.

If the press has gone short on reporting the Bank Reform here, you can get the general outline from my "Jefferson and/or Mussolini). American edtn. P. II7 (same in Eng/ edtn. Chap. XXX)

State of the Bank of the U.S. under Washington. Before Hamilton[6] and Biddle[7] had got in their dirty work.

(lines following "While the govt. remained at Philadelphia".)[8]

For the Republican party to DO anything, the sole chance is a combination on the lines of VanBuren Jackson.

You wd/ have to supply the Van B// element, the sharp definition of ideas.

No use my putting down details UNLESS you approve at least part of this letter.

1. Philip J. Burns suggests that this reference is to George Nelson Peek (1873–1943), who was head of the Agricultural Adjustment Administration for a short time in 1933 until he was removed because of disagreements with Henry Wallace (73).

2. Christopher Hollis was a British economist and biographer (Burns 70).

3. Montgomery Butchart was a British economist whose book *Money* traces three centuries of money and credit theories (Burns 73).

4. The British journalist Alfred Richard Orage (1873–1934) edited the Social Credit publication *New Age* (Burns 73).

5. Edmondo Rossoni (1884–1965) was Mussolini's minister of agriculture (Burns 69). Pound liked him for his Confucian ideas about agricultural reforms and production (Casillo 386–87).

6. During Washington's administration, Alexander Hamilton (?1753–1804) established a national fiscal system (Edwards 85).

7. The american financier Nicholas Biddle (1786–1844) was president of the Bank of the United States from 1823 to 1839. In canto 37, Pound writes about Biddle's Bank, which never came to fruition, but would have been a private bank that controlled the treasury.

8. See letter 28.

POUND TO BOTTOLFSEN

TL-2, Rapallo

20 January 1940

To His Excellency the Governor of Idaho

One spent yesterday in the knowledge of Senator Borah's probable death. Half the senate could die off without the European papers taking note of it. If I who had met him only twice and known him before that by a series of brief letters, feel a personal loss, I can well imagine the feelings of those who had known him better and on that score this note would be an intrusion, but the loss is much more than personal.

You in Idaho may feel the loss to the State very keenly, without estimating to the full what his death may mean to the Nation. You know that Idaho was more represented in the Senate than other states of equal or quintuple population. I wonder do you realize the difficulty you will have in finding another Senator to defend you as well against the foreign financial powers working through naturalized firms in Wall St.. to find another man who can hold out so strongly against the flattery of Washington D.C..

The loss of seniority you may guage. The loss of his experience may not be as apparent in Boise as it bids fair to be here in Rapallo. I can only urge you warn his successor. Warn him against tendencious news of Europe that arrives filtered through the financed and utterly mendacious press of London and Paris. Warn him against the abysmal ignorance of American history wherein OUR geneeration was brought up.

Give him Overholser's little "History of Money in the U.S.A"[1] Put that book into the high school courses in Idaho. Tell him to talk economics with Senator Bankhead (not with the Speaker of the same name).

Tell him above all to watch all monetary measures with an eye on the interest of IDAHO and the people, as distinct from the interest of money-lenders, particularly of Wall St firms having British connections. And these connections go back horribly to the bind-up of Ikleheimer in N.Y. with Rothschild in London in 1863 (and that's not the half of it. That is in fact neither the beining nor the end of it.²

It need not be forgotten that ex-senator Pope had the admirable curiosity to come over to Europe to look about for himself.. As Borah was above party, I need hardly remind you that Idaho might do worse than continue the tradition of having a man in Washington who should be blinded neither party intrigues nor flattery, and who could maintain an all too lost tradition of American statesmanship.

With expression of sympathy,
I remain yours very truly

1. Willis A. Overholser privately published the book *Short Reviews and Analysis of the History of Money in the United States* out of his law office in 1936. He sent Pound a copy, which the poet liked so much he tried to publicize it (Wilhelm 134).

2. Pound believed in a financial conspiracy centered in Wall Street and London (Casillo 380). In 1863 the National Banking Act strengthened national banks while weakening state banks. In other writings Pound refers to the collaborative efforts of banks and a letter from the Rothschild brothers that was sent to the firm of Ikleheimer, Morton, and Van der Gould in 1863 (Ahearn 153). In reference to the letter Pound comments, "It was a Rothschild who wrote 'Those few who can understand the (ursurocratic) system will be . . . busy getting profits . . . while the general public . . . will probably never suspect that the system is absolutely against their interests'" (*Selected* 311).

Appendix B:
The Meeting between the Poet and the Senator

CORKER TO PEARLMAN

TLS-4, Seattle

25 August 1980
Professor Daniel Pearlman
Department of English
University of Rhode Island
Independence Hall
Kingston, Rhode Island 02881

Dear Professor Pearlman:

    Your letter of July 31 was on my desk when I returned from vacation.

    I am glad to tell you all I remember of Pound and his meeting with Senator Borah in the fall of 1939. I hope that the recollection does not discourage your enterprise. Indeed, I do not think it should, even though I must tell you that there is reason to doubt that there ever was a genuine Pound-Borah correspondence. It should be enough for your purposes that Pound thought he corresponded with Borah. For literary purposes, at least, the prayers of St. Francis should not interest depending on (1) whether God was listening, (2) whether He sometimes or always responded, or (3) whether He exists. At least, a writer or compiler of the St. Francis prayers should not wait definitive proof about those things.

First, I was 22 years old in 1939, but I was never a "legal clerk" to the Senator. He had none. The standard complement of employees for a United States Senator was five persons, all carried on the Senate payroll as "clerk" or "assistant clerk." I was the most junior in his office: salary, $1,800 per year, which was more than enough to go to school on at George Washington University, from five to seven in the evenings. Maximum: $3,900 per year, salary of the head secretary, named Cora Rubin, who died two years ago in Boise at age of 101. Senator's salary: $10,000. I was an undergraduate, although I intended to go to law school, as I did after the Senator's death.

My duties included pasting clippings in the Senator's scrapbook (now, I have been told, at the University of Idaho's Borah Foundation); errands for Idaho constituents, performed by telephone and in person at government departments; research usually of rather a specific nature in the Senate law library or the Library of Congress, often consisting of finding some obscure quotation the Senator remembered reading which he wanted to find; miscellaneous things like driving him home at night, which was never something he asked anyone to do, but something I always wanted to do, because this was the time he either was willing to reminisce or to talk about developments in the Senate.

Senator Borah was always accessible to Idahoans (at least if they were patient), and letters from Idahoans (except from Secretaries to Chambers of Commerce) were always answered. And I think he followed a rule that no Idahoan ever expatriated himself, even if he moved to Italy, which accounts for why he found time to see Pound. But personal visitors often had to wait, at busy times, and visits were usually kept quite short—unless the visitor were someone the Senator knew—often by the device of a secretary breaking in to announce that some imaginary committee was about to have an executive session.

Pound made quite an impression on me at the time, and had a good opportunity to do so, because he returned about three times, and spent substantial time in the office (maybe 2–3 hours a visit) waiting before he was finally able to see the Senator. The bases for my impression were that Pound was the first widely known poet I had ever known, second, he was a flamboyant character actor constantly and obviously playing (or overplaying) Ezra Pound, and third, I was puzzled as I still am to know whether he was crazy.

He wore a broad-brimmed hat with a ribbon or a tassel, an open-necked shirt when open-necked shirts on Capitol Hill were not usual, and he appeared to bounce along at about four feet to a stride, announcing himself halfway through the door, "Hello, hello, hello!"

He translated everything he said into at least three languages, to make his point clear, although he knew that I was a farm boy from Idaho who spoke only English. The talk was of economics and world politics. I found his views, so far as I understood them, quite largely repulsive or incredible.

For example: Yes, speech is perfectly free in Italy. Everyone can say everything he wants, except—of course—he may be answerable for damaging falsehoods, lies . . . just like it is here.

The Italian government was the victim of prejudice in France and England—so was Germany—most of it accounted for by Jews. Particularizing about Jewish wives of British MPs and cabinet members. He usually offered specific names.

But as a performer he carried it off well. He did indeed speak poetry, rather than prose. Some of his anecdotes were about rough-cut Idahoans abroad. He believed he had important messages for Senator Borah. Maybe to Borah he listened, but my impression is that probably he listened mostly to himself.

Eventually the Senator spent perhaps 20 minutes with him. I do not remember seeing Pound on his way out, and I am quite sure I never saw him again. However, I drove the Senator home on what I believe was the same day, and I recall his two remarks:

"Do you know how that poet makes a living?"

"I think he's crazy."

There may have been a note of reproach in the latter comment. Most of what the Senator relied on his staff to do was to spare him from hoards of people, an astonishingly large percentage of whom in Senate Office Building corridors were at or beyond the edge of ordinary rationality. My impression is that Borah may or may not have known who Pound was, that he was not at all familiar with his poetry, that he did not take Pound's political and "economic" messages seriously. Indeed, Pound's anti-Semitism as it emerged from his conversation with me would have been embarrassing to the Senator, who was a leader of the fight for neutrality of the United States in European war. As Borah's Senate speech of 1937 or 1938 on Guernica shows, he was just as stoutly anti-fascist, and—characteristic of a political loner— more likely to suffer embarrassment at the hands of his friends and would-be supporters than from his enemies.

Finally, about the correspondence. My familiarity with practice in the office began in January, 1937. I was surprised to learn in 1937 that the letter which I had enterprisingly solicited in 1934 from Borah for his views on a high school debate topic bore a signature by someone else. All of his staff members signed his name to letters, imitating his signature. Usually, the reply was: "Thank you for the benefit of your views." If the Senator had taken a public position, the reply might say, "for your support." And one might add some information about the status of the issue if it were before Congress. The Senator rarely wanted to see these replies.

The Senator usually saw only a sampling of mail on most issues. I have no recollection and had not known that Pound had corresponded with him. Sometimes, however, he used a reply to a letter picked at random to state his views rather fully. Such letters might be released to the press, but many were not. Example: When castigated for supporting the nomination of Hugo Black, a former Klansman, to the Supreme Court, he prepared a speech, never delivered. Then he answered one letter something like this:

"Dear Madam:
   Thank you for your letter on tolerance. I hope you understand the meaning of the word.
                    Sincerely,
                    [signature]"

I am quite confident that a questioned documents examiner—and I think the Library of Congress may have some of this talent available—

could tell you if the Borah letters in the Pound papers are signed by Borah. The Library of Congress was responsible for the information a couple of decades ago that Madison's Notes on the constitutional convention were written on paper that was manufactured some years after the convention, although they are written in Madison's handwriting.

You may use my letter if you wish. If you quote only excerpts, however, I ask that you allow me to approve the excerpts. I do not want to be quoted out of context, and in particular, to have said even inferentially that Borah was an unlettered politician. The writers he read—again and again in many instances—were Shakespearean rather than contemporary poets. His failure to remember Pound's name may have been a momentary bit of forgetfulness, but I doubt that Ezra Pound—even though identified with Hailey, Idaho—was a name he would ever have recognized.

                Sincerely,
                Charles E. Corker
                Professor of Law

CEC:bk

Works Cited

Ahearn, Barry, ed. *Pound/Cummings: The Correspondence of Ezra Pound and E. E. Cummings.* Ann Arbor: University of Michigan Press, 1996.
"Amery, Leopold Charles." *Cambridge Biographical Dictionary.* 1990.
Ashby, LeRoy. *The Spearless Leader: Senator Borah and the Progressive Movement in the 1920's.* Urbana: University of Illinois Press, 1972.
Baer, George W. *Test Case: Italy, Ethiopia, and the League of Nations.* Stanford: Hoover Institution Press, 1976.
"Bankhead, John Hollis." *Concise Dictionary of American Biography.* 2d ed. 1977.
"Bank of the United States." *Compton's Encyclopedia.* 1995.
"Beaverbrook, Baron Max Aitken." *Cambridge Biographical Dictionary.* 1990.
"Blaine, James G." *Concise Dictionary of American Biography.* 2d ed. 1977.
Bondi, Victor. *American Decades.* Vol. 4. New York: Gale, 1995.
Borah, William. "Borah Assails Government Trends." NBC. 4 Jul. 1934. Transcript.
———. "Delegation of Power." U.S. Senate. 17 May 1934. Transcript.
———. "Fascism." U.S. Senate. 6 May 1937. Transcript.
———. "Fascism." U.S. Senate. 23 June 1937. Transcript.
———. "Radio Speech of Hon. WM. E. Borah." CBS. 22 Mar. 1934. Transcript.
———. "Senator Borah Discusses 'Our Foreign Policy.'" CBS. 22 Sept. 1935. Transcript.
———. "Washington's Foreign Policy." CBS. 22 Feb. 1936. Transcript.
"Borah, William E." *American National Biography.* 1999.

"Borah, William E." *Concise Dictionary of American Biography.* 2d ed. 1977.
Brooks, John. *Once in Golconda: A True Drama of Wall Street, 1920–1938.* New York: Harper, 1969.
Burns, Philip J., ed. *"Dear Uncle George": The Correspondence between Ezra Pound and Congressman Tinkham of Massachusetts.* Orono, Maine: National Poetry Foundation, 1996.
Carpenter, Humphrey. *A Serious Character: The Life of Ezra Pound.* Boston: Houghton Mifflin, 1988.
Casillo, Robert. *The Genealogy of Demons: Anti-Semitism, Fascism, and the Myths of Ezra Pound.* Evanston, Ill.: Northwestern University Press, 1988.
"Chamberlain, Neville." *Dictionary of National Biography.* 1974.
"Chavez, Dennis." *American National Biography.* 1999.
"Cleveland, Grover." *Concise Dictionary of American Biography.* 2d ed. 1977.
Cong. Rec. 27 Jan. 1934: 1476–77.
Darkwah, R. H. Kofi. *Shewa, Menilek, and the Ethiopian Empire: 1813–1889.* London: Heinemann, 1975.
"Darley, Henry." *Who Was Who.* 1920.
"Drummond, James Eric." *Concise Dictionary of National Biography.* 1982.
"Eden, Anthony." *Concise Dictionary of National Biography.* 1982.
Edwards, John Hamilton, and William W. Vasse. *Annotated Index to the Cantos of Ezra Pound.* Berkeley: University of California Press, 1957.
"Ezra Pound Papers." Beinecke Information Page. 18 Aug. 2000. <http://webtext.library.yale.edu/sgml2html/beinecke.pound1.sgm.html>.
Farago, Ladislas. *Abyssinia on the Eve.* New York: Putnam, 1935.
"Fighting Line." *New Democracy* 1 Dec. 1935: 122–23.
Fisher, Irving. *Stabilizing the Dollar: A Plan to Stabilize the General Price Level without Fixing Individual Prices.* New York: Macmillan, 1920.
Flory, Wendy Stallard. *The American Ezra Pound.* New Haven: Yale University Press, 1989.
Hardie, Frank. *The Abyssinian Crisis.* London: Batsford, 1974.
Harris, Brice, Jr. *The United States and the Italo-Ethiopian Crisis.* Stanford University Press, 1964.
"Hawkins, Sir John." *The Dictionary of National Biography.* 1917.
Heymann, David C. *Ezra Pound: The Last Rower, a Political Profile.* New York: Viking, 1976.
"History of Skoda." Skoda Information Page. 18 July 2000. <http://www.skoda.cz/eng/historie_indexnn.htm>.
"Hull, Cordell." *Dictionary of American Biography.* Supp. 5. 1977.

Kennedy, David M. *Freedom from Fear: The American People in Depression and War, 1929–1945*. The Oxford History of the United States. Vol 9. New York: Oxford University Press, 1999.
"Knox, Philander Chase." *American National Biography*. 1999.
Laughlin, James. *Pound as Wuz: Essays and Lectures on Ezra Pound*. St. Paul, Minn.: Graywolf, 1987.
Leuchtenburg, William E. *The FDR Years: On Roosevelt and His Legacy*. New York: Columbia University Press, 1995.
"Lodge, Henry Cabot." *American National Biography*. 1999.
McKenna, Marian C. *Borah*. Ann Arbor: University of Michigan Press, 1961.
Norman, Charles. *Ezra Pound*. New York: Macmillan, 1960.
"Norman, Sir Montagu." *Concise Dictionary of National Biography*. 1982.
Olson, James S. *Historical Dictionary of the New Deal: From Inauguration to Preparation for War*. Westport, Conn.: Greenwood, 1985.
Pearlman, Daniel. "Fighting the World: The Letters of Ezra Pound to Senator William E. Borah of Idaho." *Paideuma* 12 (1983): 419–26.
Pound, Ezra. "Ahead." *New Democracy* 15 May 1934: 5.
———. "American Notes." *New English Weekly* 10 Jan. 1935: 270.
———. "American Notes." *New English Weekly* 16 May 1935: 85.
———. "American Notes." *New English Weekly* 6 June 1935: 145.
———. "American Notes." *New English Weekly* 13 June 1935: 165.
———. "American Notes." *New English Weekly* 4 July 1935: 225.
———. "American Notes." *New English Weekly* 11 July 1935: 245.
———. "American Notes." *New English Weekly* 25 July 1935: 285.
———. "American Notes." *New English Weekly* 12 Sept. 1935: 345.
———. "American Notes." *New English Weekly* 21 Nov. 1935: 105.
———. "American Notes." *New English Weekly* 12 Mar. 1936: 425.
———. "American Notes." *New English Weekly* 2 Apr. 1936: 489.
———. "As to Sprague." *New Democracy* 1 Feb. 1934: 3.
———. *The Cantos of Ezra Pound*. New York: New Directions, 1972.
———. "Economic Light from Parnassus." *New York Herald* [Paris] 23 Aug. 1933: 4.
———. "From Far Away Italy Come Greetings to Hailey Folks." *Hailey Times* 18 June 1931: 38–39.
———. "Gold and Work." Trans. John Drummond. Pound, *Selected* 336–51.
———. "Hidden Govt." *New Democracy* 15 Apr. 1935: 67.
———. "History and Ignorance." *New English Weekly* 25 July 1935: 287.
———. *Impact: Essays on Ignorance and the Decline of American Civilization*. Ed. Noel Stock. Chicago: Regnery, 1960.
———. "Jacques Duboin and the Ligue du Droit au Travail." *New English Weekly* 20 Feb. 1936: 92–93.

―――. *Jefferson and/or Mussolini; L'idea Statale; Fascism as I Have Seen It.* New York: Liveright, 1936.
―――. Letter. *New Democracy* 1 June 1934: 11.
―――. Letter. *New Democracy* 1 Nov. 1934: 87.
―――. Letter. *New English Weekly* 31 May 1934: 167.
―――. "More Light, Bert." *New York Herald* [Paris] 23 Oct. 1934: 4.
―――. "Packages without Label." *New York Herald* [Paris] 11 Oct. 1934: 4.
―――. "Possibilities of Economics." *New York Herald* [Paris] 30 Aug. 1933: 4.
―――. *Selected Prose: 1909–1965.* New York: New Directions Press, 1973.
―――. "Stamp Script." *New English Weekly* 26 Oct. 1933: 31–32.
―――. "Time Lag in the American Wilderness." *New English Weekly* 6 Dec. 1934: 175.
―――. "Volitionist Economics." *New Democracy* 15 Nov. 1934: 105.
―――. "Who Gets It?" *New Democracy* 1 Dec. 1935: 120–22.
―――. "Woodward (W.E.) Historian." *New English Weekly* 4 Feb. 1937: 329–30.
"Quay, Matthew." *Concise Dictionary of American Biography.* 2d ed. 1977.
Redman, Tim. *Ezra Pound and Italian Fascism.* Cambridge: Cambridge University Press, 1991.
Roberts, John G. *Mitsui: Three Centuries of Japanese Business.* New York: Weatherhill, 1973.
Roosevelt, Franklin D. *The Public Papers and Addresses of Franklin D. Roosevelt.* Vol. 4. New York: Random, 1938. 5 vols.
"Rothschild Family." *Compton's Encyclopedia.* 1995.
Said, Edward, "Reflections on Exile." *One World, Many Cultures.* Ed. Stuart Hirschberg. 2d ed. Needham Heights, Mass.: Allyn and Bacon, 1995. 447–53.
Sawinski, Diane M., and Wendy H. Mason, eds. *Encyclopedia of Global Industries.* New York: Gale, 1996.
Sayers, R. S. *The Bank of England: 1891–1944.* 2 vols. London: Cambridge University Press, 1976.
Schlesinger, Arthur M. *The Coming of the New Deal.* Vol. 2 of *The Age of Roosevelt.* Boston: Riverside-Houghton Mifflin, 1959.
―――. *The Crisis of the Old Order: 1919–1933.* Vol. 1 of *The Age of Roosevelt.* Boston: Riverside-Houghton Mifflin, 1957.
―――. *The Politics of Upheaval.* Vol. 3 of *The Age of Roosevelt.* Boston: Riverside-Houghton Mifflin, 1960.
"Singolare Progetto Perfavorire la Rinascita Economica del Principato di Monaco." *Lavoro* 10 May 1934: 9.

"Smith, Alfred Emanuel." *Concise Dictionary of American Biography.* 2d ed. 1977.

"Sprague, Oliver Mitchell Wentworth." *Dictionary of American Biography.* Supp. 5. 1977.

Terrell, Carroll F. *A Companion to the Cantos of Ezra Pound.* Berkeley: University of California Press, 1980.

"Townsend, Francis Everett." *American National Biography.* 1999.

Tryphonopoulos, Demetres P., and Leon Surette, eds. *"I Cease Not to Yowl": Ezra Pound's Letters to Oliva Rossetti Agresti.* Urbana: University of Illinois Press, 1998.

Verdad, S. "European Affairs." *New English Weekly* 25 Jul. 1935: 288–89.

Vinson, John Chalmers. *William E. Borah and the Outlawry of War.* Athens: University of Georgia Press, 1957.

Walkiewicz, E. P., and Hugh Witemeyer, eds. *Ezra Pound and Senator Bronson Cutting: A Political Correspondence, 1930–1935.* Albuquerque: University of New Mexico Press, 1995.

Wilhelm, J. J. *Ezra Pound: The Tragic Years: 1925–1972.* University Park: Pennsylvania State University Press, 1994.

Wilson, Derek. *Rothschild: The Wealth and Power of a Dynasty.* New York: Scribner's, 1988.

Wilson, R. McNair. *The Defeat of Debt.* London: Routledge, 1935.

Witemeyer, Hugh, ed. *Pound/Williams: Selected Letters of Ezra Pound and William Carlos Williams.* New York: New Directions, 1996.

Index

Abyssinia, invasion of, xx–xxi, 41n, 47n, 48n, 53n; Borah on, xxiii, 50n; Franklin Roosevelt on, 43n; Pound on, 40, 42, 46, 47, 49, 53n, 55
Agricultural Adjustment Act, 36n
American Liberty League, 23n
Amery, Leopold, 49, 50n
Angell, Sir Norman, 36, 37n, 49
Anti-Comintern Pact, 41n
Anti-Semitism: Borah on, 82; Father Charles Coughlin on, 33n; Pound on, 3n, 28, 36n, 58, 59n, 65, 68, 81
Austrian National Bank, xvii

Bankhead, John, 2n, 6, 20, 52, 77
Bankhead-Pettengill bill, xviii, 1, 2n, 5, 6
Bank of England, 47n, 65n
Bank of France: members of, 18n, 41n, 47n; Pound on, 5, 22, 40, 46, 54
Bank of the United States, 76n
Baruch, Bernard: political career of, 3n; Pound on, 2, 3n, 6, 28, 32, 35, 67
Beaverbrook, Baron Max Aitken, 20, 23n, 65
Beckett, Sir Gervase, 52, 53n, 58
Berle, Adolf, 21, 23n
Biddle, Nicholas, 76
Blaine, James, 15, 16n, 28, 34
Borah, William: on American Liberty League, 23n; on banking system, 15n; as Chairman of Senate Foreign Relations Committee, xix, xxiv; on distribution, 12n, 13n; on expatriatism, 80; on fascism, x, xxii, 19n, 27n, 82; on Italian invasion of Abyssinia, 50n; on League of Nations, xxiii–xxiv, 40n; on neutrality of the United States, 82, xxiii–xxiv; as part of Progressive movement, xxii, xxv, 3n; political career of, xxii; presidential nomination of, x, 10n, 75; on purchasing power, 7n, 12n; on Reciprocal Trade Agreements Act,

10n; reputation of, xxiv, xxv;
on Russia, 18n; on Treaty of
Versailles, xxiii; visit with
Pound, xxi, 79–83; on war, 42n
Brain Trust, 23n, 30, 31n, 57n
Bullett, William, 68, 69n
Burke, Edmund, xxiii
Burns, Philip, xvii
Butchart, Montgomery, 75, 76n
Butler, Nicholas: career of, 16n;
Pound on, 15, 17, 22, 29, 46

Carnegie Endowment for International Peace, 14, 15n, 16n
Chamberlain, Neville, xxi, 49, 50n
Chavez, Dennis, 35, 37n
Child labor, 60, 61n, 72n
Churchill, Winston, 41n
Cleveland, Grover, 28, 34
Cohrsson, Hans, 35, 36n, 37n
Consumption, xxi, 31, 64n
Coolidge, Calvin, 51
Corriere della Sera, 63, 64n
Il Corriere Mercantile, 58, 59n
Coughlin, Father Charles, 32, 33n, 36n, 62
Credit, 11n, 20, 28, 74, 76n
Cutting, Bronson: career of, 35, 37n; correspondence with Pound, 7n, 23n, 64n; Pound on, 9, 17, 21, 25, 26, 38; and Progressive movement, 3n; on purchasing power, 10n

Daladier, Edouard, 62, 64n, 75
Darley, Henry, 49, 50n
Defeat of Debt (Wilson), 52, 53n
Delaisi, Francis, 40, 41n
de Rachewiltz, Mary, ix, xv
Deterding, Sir Henry, 17, 18n

de Wendel, François, 17, 18n, 54
Distribution: Borah on, 12n, 31n; Pound on, 17, 22, 25, 31
Dividend: definition of, xvi; Huey Long on, 38n; Pound on, 3n, 12n, 17, 26, 28–29, 30, 32, 60
Dole, 60, 61n
Douglas, C. H.: dinner for, 20, 21, 23n, 38; economic theory of, 3n; meeting with Pound, xvi; Pound on, 2, 12, 17, 22, 25–26, 30, 35, 39n, 75
Drummond, James, 47, 48n
Duboin, Jacques, 62, 64n, 75

Eden, Anthony, 46, 47n, 50n, 52
Emerson, Ralph Waldo, xxiii
Evening Standard, 52
Expatriatism, xvii–xix, xxi
Ezekiel, Mordecai, 35, 36n

Farley, James, xviii, 9, 10n
Fascism: Borah on, xxii, 27n; Franklin Roosevelt on, 54; Pound on, xx, 26, 28, 60
Fischer, Irving, 33n, 35, 36n, 37n, 57n
Fixed prices, 25, 26
Food, destruction of, 30, 31n
Ford, Henry, 62, 75

Geneva, Switzerland, 46, 48n, 49, 50n, 54
Gesell, Silvio, xvii, 2, 20, 23n, 35
Gold standard: Borah on, xxiv; debate over, 2n, 3n, 11n, 37n, 47n
Gregory, Sir Theodore, 46, 47n
Griffiths, Arthur, 30, 31n
Grigg, Sir Edward William, 49, 50n

Hailey, Idaho, 5, 6n, 71, 73, 83
Hamilton, Alexander, 76
Harding, Warren, xxii, 2, 3n, 6, 23n, 51
Hawkins, Sir John, 55, 56n
Hitler, Adolf, 48n, 62, 75
Hoare, Sir Samuel, xx, 41n, 52, 53n, 55
Hollis, Christopher, 74, 76n
Hoover, Herbert: Borah on, 34; political career of, 3n, 15n; Pound on, 2, 3n, 6, 14, 30, 32, 46, 51, 52, 62
House of Rothschild, 68, 78
Hull, Cordell: political career of, 10n, 41n, 43n; Pound on, 9, 46, 54, 55

Ickes, Harold, 34, 36n
Industrial Advisory Board, 13
Insull, Samuel, 14, 15n
International Herald Tribune, 12, 14, 28, 34

Jackson, Andrew, 76
Jefferson, Thomas, 21, 44, 59, 63
J. P. Morgan and Company, 15n, 47n

Kemmerer, E. W., 3n
Kennedy, Joseph, 68, 69n
Kitson, Arthur, 5, 6n
Knox, Philander, 66, 67n
Kreuger, Ivar, 5, 7n
Kristeva, Julia, xx

Lamont, Thomas, 14, 15n, 30, 63
Landon, Alfred, 52, 53n, 57, 66
Lansbury, George, 49, 50n
Larkin, James Crate, 62, 64n
Laval, Pierre, 54, 56n

Lavoro, 17, 18n
League for the Right to Work, 62, 64n, 75
League of Nations: Borah on, xxiii–xxiv, 40n; on Italian-Abyssinian crisis, xx, 41n, 48n, 50n, 53n; Pound on, 42, 49, 66
Lehman, Herbert, 35, 36n
Lewis, Wyndham, xii
Lippmann, Walter, 35, 36n
Lodge, Henry Cabot, 66, 67n
Long, Huey, 32, 34, 38
Lorimer, George, 57

Manchester Guardian, 52
Marx, Karl, 72n
Mellon, Andrew, 2, 3n, 14, 17, 32, 65
Mencken, H. L., 8n
Meyer, Eugene, 10, 11n, 21
Moley, Raymond, 31n
Money, Chiozza, 49, 50n
Morgan, J. P., 7n, 46, 47n
Morgenthau, Henry, Jr.: political career of, 47n, 59n; Pound on, 46, 58, 65, 67
Morgenthau, Henry, Sr., 28, 29n, 35, 58, 59n
Munitions: Birmingham Small Arms, 52, 53n; Borah on, xxiv, 36n; Mitsui, 5, 7n, 22, 49, 50, 55; Nye Commission, 46, 47n, 50n; Pound on, xxi, 1, 46, 49; Schneider, 22, 23n; Skoda, 68; Vickers-Armstrong, 22, 23n; Whitworth, 52, 53n
Murray, Gilbert, 49, 50n
Mussolini, Benito: correspondence with Pound, xvi, 2n, 36n; on invasion of Abyssinia, xx–xxi, 40n, 53n; Pound on,

xx–xxi, 26, 28, 29, 42, 53n,
55, 75

National Banking Act, 78n
Neimeyer, Otto Ernst, 65
Neutrality Act, 41n, 43n
New Deal, 2n, 36n, 37n, 73n
New York Times, 5, 9
Nicholas II (Nicholas Romanov), 22, 23n
Norman, Sir Montagu, 46, 47n, 65
Nye, Gerald, 46, 47n, 49, 50n
Nyland, W. A., 62, 64n

Orage, Alfred, 75, 76n
Overholser, Willis, 77, 78n

Partaggio, 60, 61n
Passport Control Act, 7n, 71–72
Pecora Committee, 15n
Peek, George Nelson, 74, 76n
Perkins, Frances, 67
Pettengill, Samuel, 2n
Pope, James, 73, 78
Pound, Ezra, works: *ABC of Economics*, 20; *Cantos*, xx, xxi, 2n, 8n, 21, 22, 23n; in *Esquire*, 55, 56n; *Jefferson and/or Mussolini*, xxi, 21, 59, 63, 64n, 76; in *New Democracy*, 17, 20, 22, 23, 24n, 52; in *New English Weekly*, 20, 22, 47; in *New York Herald*, 5; "Volitionist Economics," 60, 61
Pound, Homer, 5, 34, 47, 73
Public Works Administration, 36n
Purchasing power: Borah on, 7n, 12n; Cutting on, 10n; and Franklin Roosevelt, 24n, 60n; and Irving Fisher, 33n, 37n; Pound on, 6, 9–10, 17–18, 22, 24n, 34, 35, 60, 61n; Social Credit, xvi–xvii, 3n

Quay, Matthew, 34, 36n

Redman, Tim, xvi, xx
Reid, Ogden Mills, 35, 36n
Republican party: and Borah, ix, x, xxii, 38, 46, 51, 58, 63, 66, 73; members at Cutting's party for Douglas, 22; Pound on, 3n, 14–15, 28, 31, 35, 54, 57, 67, 76; and Theodore Roosevelt Jr., 23n
Riddell, Walter, 49, 50n
Rist, Charles, 46, 47n
Rocke, Cyril, 46, 47
Rome-Berlin Axis agreement, 41n
Roosevelt, Franklin: and Brain Trust, 23n, 30, 31n, 57n; on fascism, 54; on invasion of Abyssinia, 43n; political career of, ix, 2n, 38n, 41n, 59n; Pound on, 6, 12, 14, 21–23, 28, 29, 33n, 35, 42, 44, 51, 58, 65, 66–67; on purchasing power, 24n, 60n
Roosevelt, Theodore, Jr., 22, 23n
Rossoni, Edmondo, 75, 76n
Rothermore, Viscount, 20, 23n
Runciman, Walter, 65

Said, Edward, xix
Sanctions imposed on Italy, xx, 41n, 43n, 47n, 50n; Pound on, xxi, 47, 49, 56
Sassoon family, 58, 59n
Saturday Evening Post, 5, 7n, 57n
Selassie, Emperor Haile, 41n, 50n

Senate Foreign Relations Committee, xix, xxiv, 67n
Share Our Wealth Society, 33n
Silver, xxiv, 14, 52, 53n
Smith, Alfred, 1, 2n, 62
Social Credit: Alberta's political party, 38n; definition of, xvi, 3n; National Social Credit Association, 64n; Pound on, 31n, 38, 39n, 60, 64n; publications about, 76n
Sprague, Oliver, 1, 2n, 5, 9, 21
Stable Money (Fisher and Cohrsson), 35, 37n
Stamp scrip: in Bankhead-Pettengill bill, xviii, 1, 2n, 5, 6; definition of, xvii, 2n; and Italy, 18n; Pound on, 1, 2, 6, 20, 21, 22, 30, 32, 61n, 64n
Stein, Gertrude, ix
Straus, Jesse, 58, 59n, 63
Swope, Gerald, 10, 11n, 21

Taft, William, xxii
Tannery, Jean, 47, 58
Thyssen, 22, 23n
Time and Tide, 36, 37n
Tinkham, George: correspondence with Pound, xix; political career of, 63n; Pound on, 16n, 62, 63, 66–67, 74–75

Townsend, Francis, 52, 53n
Treaty of Versailles, xxiii
Tugwell, Rexford, 51, 53n, 57

Usury, 50, 54–55, 58, 60, 78n

Van Buren, Martin, 21, 22, 76
Vanderlip, Frank, 32, 33n

Wallace, Henry: political career of, 31n, 36n, 57n, 76n; Pound on, 57, 67
Warburg, James P., 35, 36n
Warren, George, 33n
Whitney, George, 14, 15n
Whitney, Richard, 14, 15n
Wiggin, Albert, 6, 8n, 14
Wilson, McNair, 52, 53n
Wilson, Woodrow: political career of, 7n, 28, 29n; Pound on, 3n, 6, 7n, 71
Witemeyer, Hugh, xiii
Wood, Charles Erskine Scott, 71, 72n
Woodin, William, 2n, 6, 8n
Woodward, W. E., 13, 21, 25
Wörgl, Austria, xvii, 6, 8n
World War I, 7n, 18n, 43n, 47n, 49n
World War II, 41n, 69n

SARAH C. HOLMES is an English instructor at the University of Rhode Island. She is currently completing her dissertation, "Leftist Literature and the Ideology of Eugenics during the American Depression."

DANIEL PEARLMAN is the author of *The Barb of Time: On the Unity of Ezra Pound's Cantos.*

Typeset in 9.5/13 Trump Mediaeval
Designed by Copenhaver Cumpston
Composed by Celia Shapland
for the University of Illinois Press
Manufactured by Maple-Vail Book Manufacturing Group

University of Illinois Press
1325 South Oak Street
Champaign, IL 61820-6903
www.press.uillinois.edu